[redacted]

PEDAGOGY LEADS TECHNOLOGY

ONLINE LEARNING AND TEACHING IN HIGHER EDUCATION: NEW TECHNOLOGIES, NEW PEDAGOGIES

EDITED BY
ARIANNE ROURKE AND KATHRYN COLEMAN

PEDAGOGY LEADS TECHNOLOGY

ONLINE LEARNING AND TEACHING IN HIGHER EDUCATION: NEW TECHNOLOGIES, NEW PEDAGOGIES

EDITED BY
ARIANNE ROURKE AND KATHRYN COLEMAN

Common Ground

First published in Champaign, Illinois in 2011
by Common Ground Publishing LLC
as part of the Technology and Society series

Library of Congress Cataloging-in-Publication Data

Pedagogy leads technology : online learning and teaching in higher education : new technologies, new pedagogies / edited by Arianne Rourke and Kathryn Coleman.

p. cm.

ISBN 978-1-86335-914-6 ((pbk) : alk. paper) -- ISBN 978-1-86335-915-3 ((pdf))

1. Education, Higher--Computer-assisted instruction. 2. Education, Higher--Effect of technological innovations on. 3. Educational technology I. Rourke, Arianne. II. Coleman, Kathryn.

LB2395.7.P44 2011
378.1'734--dc22

2011007343

Cover image: Phillip Kalantzis-Cope

Table of Contents

Part III : Online Collaborative Learning

Part IV : Conclusion

Acknowledgments

This edited collection of articles is evidence of both the editors and author's commitment to utilising technology to enhance student learning in higher education. It is with pleasure that the editors gathered some of the leading pedagogy and technology researchers together in one edited book whose contribution to the literature showcases how pedagogy can lead technology in higher education teaching, learning and assessment.

We would like to thank the contributing authors Deborah West, Linda E. Robinson, Robert D. Hannafin, David R. Parker, Peter Mark Jansson, Kate Thomson, Boon-Kiang Tan, Christopher Brook, Carmen Pérez Basanta, Mark Mabrito, Marlo Ransdell, Trevor Nesbit, Jason Black, Lois W. Hawkes and James A West for keeping to deadlines and for allowing their work to not only be further shared but also to add to the literature in the field. Thanks also to Kathryn Otto and Common Grounds Publishing for supporting this Edited Collection.

We would also like to thank our families for their continuing love and support.

Foreword

This book provides case study examples of recent research that acknowledges that pedagogy should continue to drive technology. Following the themes of interactive technologies for learning, learning through online communities, online collaborative learning and reflecting on reflective practice the editors seek to exemplify an edited selection of multi disciplinary International award finalists from the International Journal of Technology, Knowledge and Society. The research studies showcased in this book examine pedagogical change and the scholarship of teaching in a practical application.

In education it is now acknowledged that 21st Century students use social media and mobile devices to learn, read, talk and organize their learning. Educators have to deal with this generational shift, digital wisdom and new technological literacies by engaging the digitally literate online through technologically enhanced learning. The real classroom elearning case studies presented provide useful exemplars for tertiary educators on how teaching practice can be turned into scholarly research, an important objective of many 21st Century Universities.

Arianne Rourke and Kathryn Coleman

Editors Biography Notes

Arianne Jennifer Rourke

Dr. Arianne Rourke is a Senior Lecturer at College of Fine Arts, the University of New South Wales, Australia. Her research interests are in on-line learning and teaching expert/novice differences, visual literacy and the application of Cognitive load theory to improving instructional design in higher education. Specifically her research has focused on the area of improving the teaching of undergraduate design history and Postgraduate arts administration towards the long-term retention of learning. Dr Rourke has presented at many International higher education conferences and has published extensively. She has over 19 years experience teaching undergraduate and Postgraduate tertiary students in design and the arts. She holds the following degrees: Bachelor of Arts (Visual Arts), *AMCAE*; Bachelor of Education (Art), *SCAE*; Master of Arts (History), *UNSW*; Master of Arts (Hons) *Macq*; Master of Higher Education, *UNSW*; Doctor of Education, *UNSW* and is currently completing a Master of Philosophy in Higher Education at UNSW.

Kathryn Sara Coleman

Kathryn Coleman has worked for many years as a visual arts teacher in high schools. Her research specifically focuses on increasing the integration of web 2.0 and mobile technologies into the artworld and educational setting, and examining both pedagogical and social spaces and the implications of social networking into Secondary art education. Kathryn Coleman has presented at a number of International e-learning conferences and co-authored many papers on digital scaffolding, calibrated peer review, blogs in higher education and micro-blogs in secondary art education. She is currently an Educational Designer at Learning and Teaching at the University of New South Wales, Australia.

Contributor Biography

Dr. Carmen Pérez Basanta is a senior lecturer (University of Granada) where she teaches Applied Linguistics. Her research interests include lexis, corpus linguistic and CALL.

Dr. Jason Black has a Ph.D. in Computer Science from Florida State University, and been at FAMU since 2000. His interests include Collaborative Mobile Learning, Gaming for Learning, and Education Technology.

Professor Chris Brook is the Director, Quality Enhancement for Curtin University. He was previously the Dean of Teaching and Learning at Curtin Business School and the Head of the School Regional Remote and e-Learning, where he managed Curtin's regional education program, flexible learning program as well as Distance Education and Open Universities Australia engagement. He has been awarded for his teaching and research and his research interests include teaching practices, online learning and learning communities.

Robert D. Hannafin is the Dean of the College of Education and Information Sciences at Long Island University, CW Post Campus. Prior to joining LIU, he was on the Learning and Development team at Pricewaterhouse-Coopers, and before that on the faculty of three universities specializing in instructional technology and teacher preparation. He has researched interactive learning environments and issues surrounding effective integration of technology in K-12 classrooms.

Dr. Lois W. Hawkes is co-director of the satellite facility of the High-performance Computing & Simulation Research Laboratory (HCS). This lab was established in 1993 by Dr. Alan George to investigate a wide variety of topics in high-performance computing and communications, including computer networks and architecture, parallel computing, distributed computing, and fault-tolerant computing.

Dr. Peter Mark Jansson is an Associate Professor in Electrical and Computer Engineering at Rowan University in Glassboro, NJ USA. His research and teaching areas include DC/AC networks, power systems, advanced and renewable energy technologies (specifically photovoltaics and wind systems)as well as Mach's Principle. He is also President and Principal Consultant for Integrated Systems an engineering firm specializing in renewable energy project engineering and optimization. He has published on many topics including active learning technologies, renewable energy projects and student clinic experiences. He spent nearly 20 years in the electric power industry before completing graduate work on innovation in the electric sector. He continues to involve students in discovery-driven clinic experiences as part of their graduate and undergraduate educational experiences.

Dr. Mark Mabrito has been a faculty member since 1989 at Purdue University Calumet where he teaches courses in new media, web design, and professional writing. His research interests include online learning, usability, and immersive virtual environments.

Trevor Nesbit is an Information Systems Lecturer at the University of Canterbury (Christchurch, New Zealand) and has a multi-disciplinary background that includes undergraduate majors in Mathematics, Computer Science, Operations Research and Accounting; a masters degree in Management and is currently researching towards a doctorate in Education. His teaching areas include Software Development and Accounting Information Systems and has published research in Knowledge Management; Technology in Education and Social Media.

David R. Parker, Ph.D. earned his doctorate in Special Education (emphasis: postsecondary services) at the University of Connecticut. He has coordinated disability services for college students with LD and/or ADHD at the University of North Carolina at Chapel Hill, UConn, and Washington University in St. Louis. David is also a research associate, most recently for Wayne State University where he helped a team conduct the first national (U.S.) study of ADD college coaching. His is currently in private practice at CRG in Indianapolis, a diagnostic and treatment center for individuals with learning and mood disorders.

Marlo Ransdell's work is in the appropriate use of online technologies for interior design and related applied arts fields.

Linda E. Robinson is the Coordinator for Library/Media Services for the Mansfield Public Schools. She is currently a doctoral candidate PhD candidate in Adult Learning in the Department of Educational Leadership at the University of Connecticut.

Dr Tan is a Senior Lecturer at Curtin University's Centre for International Health. She teaches in the Masters program and supervises research students. She is Director of the Curtin University's Faculty of Health Sciences Go Global program which is an international and interpr of essional clinical fieldwork program.

Kate Thomson is a PhD candidate and Postgraduate Fellow at the University of Sydney's central academic development unit, the Institute for Teaching and Learning (ITL). She has worked at the Australian Learning and Teaching Council on the Teaching Quality Indicators Project and at the ITL as a Project Officer on the National Graduate Attributes Project. She teaches on professional development courses for academics and contributes to the development of resources to support effective teaching and learning in higher education. Her PhD is titled 'The nature of informal academic discourse on university teaching', and through this, she seeks to explore informal conversations on the topic of teaching, with the intention of contributing to our understanding of the variation across departments in a single research-intensive university.

Associate Professor Deborah West (BA, MSW, PhD) is the *Director of Education and Training Development* at *Charles Darwin University* in the Northern Territory of Australia. After completing her social work training, Deborah worked as a social work practitioner in both the government and non-government sectors and as a policy officer in the Australian Government. She has over 15 years experience in higher education teaching across several disciplines and Universities and a track record of research and scholarship in the area of teaching and learning including post graduate research into lifelong learning and the use of technology.

Jim West is an Associate Professor in Instructional Design and Technology at Western Illinois University, where he teaches courses in distance learning and interactive learning technologies.

Introduction

Learning to learn online

Kathryn Coleman and Arianne Rourke

Being teachers, educators and facilitators' in the twenty first century, we have noticed the changes to education. The cyclical changes and approaches to pedagogy, curriculum, assessment, research and teaching tools. Being mothers, we have experienced the changing role of technology through our children and the new role technology now plays in non-formal learning spaces. We have seen our children add applications to our iPhones and play their Internet games, make movies and manipulate photographs on the computer without any formal learning having taken place. We have witnessed students with access to technology have the world at their fingertips. Our children and many of our students are digitally aware as Deborah West confers because of access, knowledge and money. They have not faced digital exclusion due to lack of Internet access, lack of infrastructure in their homes or broader social inequities. Our digitally literate children have been as Deborah West examines, included in the digitised society because they have a range of skills that allow for access and lifelong learning opportunities. This edited collection of papers seeks to exemplify the ideological position taken by the editors that pedagogy leads technology. Educators need to approach online learning and teaching from the perspective that the pedagogy drives the technology not the other way around.

The integration of the Internet and mobile learning devices in higher education blended and face-to-face (f2f) teaching and learning is not a 21st century invention (Rourke & Coleman, 2010b). Teachers and instructors have always sought the best technologies for their students in order to offer engaging learning pedagogies with the most recent forms of technological tools. There has however, been a shift in the student's use of technology, with recent literature purporting the millennial students desire to learn anywhere, any time to fit learning into their schedules (McLoughlin & Lee, 2009). Prensky's (2001) own reference to the 'digital native' and 'digital immigrant' led educators' into a self reflective mode of thought, believing they had been left behind, having ignored the opportunity of integrating new eLearning material and devices into the classroom to ignite their students learning (Rourke & Coleman, 2010a). This current generation of learners' in the western capitalist world has grown up with the Internet, digital technologies and second and third generation mobile phones. As West confers in "Lenses for Digital Inclusion" however, many have been socially excluded.

Deborah West examines the notion of the digital divide not from Prensky's perspective of generation and age, on the contrary, through a social work framework that allows for an investigation into the issues of social exclusion in the digitised society. West examines the digital divide through DiMaggio and Hargittai's (2002) model of dimensions:

1. "Technical means: software, hardware, connection quality,
2. autonomy of use: location of access, freedom to use for own purposes,
3. use of patterns: types of use of internet,
4. social support networks: availability of assistance if needed, size of network, and
5. skill: one's own ability to use the medium effectively".

The framework offers insight into the barriers those sectors of the community face on a number of levels, either because of financial, social, educational, geographical or generational difference. This research focuses on life long learning and the nature of digitised knowledge and the larger implications of how "technology is associated with power and that blocks to power are imposed and compound to create further disadvantage" (p.15).

It is now evident in higher education that student's technological capabilities and levels of ownership are disparate. Learning to learn online inclusively requires a more level playing field for learning opportunities to be more evenly spread. Many students have only been introduced to technology as a learning device upon entering university, only in the last few years have they experienced Learning Management Systems (LMS) in schools in Australia. The challenge for 21st century educators is to teach, instruct and facilitate course material, meet the outcomes and assess for learning all while teaching students to 'learn to learn' online simultaneously. As West advocates, "knowledge is power and awareness of technology is more likely to lead the individual to being able to make an informed choice about the pursuit and application of the technology" (p.19).

Many children and adults in developed countries do spend enormous amounts of time online, chatting, tweeting and many 'googling' the answers to everything through mobile learning devices such as smart-phones and net-books. The assumption by educators in higher education that a generational digital divide was to blame for student's disengagement from face-to-face (f2f) teaching methods and that they want to learn online because they are 'digitally native' (Prensky, 2001) is only beginning to be questioned. As Robinson, Hannafin and Parker confer, one of the biggest challenges for online educators' is an understanding of the learner's needs, learning and pedagogy, specifically for online learning.

Engaging student centred learning spaces and environments whether f2f or online trigger cooperative learning techniques that can enhance and engage student learning. Collaborative learning online takes a different approach, specifically because of the asynchronous nature of communication. Robinson, Hannafin and Parker discuss the design and delivery of a course to support blended learning within a community of practice (CoP) bound as Wilson (2004) supported by expectations of contribution and time. As supported by the contributing authors, learning to learn requires specific teaching to the environment, an extra challenge in education. Provision of a moderator online provides support and scaffolding for student learning needs. The authentic tasks discussed by Robinson, Hannafin and Parker has real world context, further enabled by the CoP this research exemplifies the ideology of this edited collection of papers, pedagogy leading the technology.

Effective and engaging educators seek to embed and integrate learning experience and knowledge building into the pedagogy (Rourke & Coleman, 2011). Student centred learning is typified by student and teacher knowledge sharing, (McLoughlin, 2002; Biggs, 1999) where student learning that has real world relevance (Cronin, 1993; Jonassen, 1991) is supported by the teaching and authentic assessment (Herrington, Oliver & Reeves, 2010). As Robinson, Hannafin and Parker confer, to "engage all students, further research is needed" to explore other ways to modify course design to encourage student risk taking in online environments (p.44) and promote satisfaction in online and blended learning spaces. This paradigm shift as positioned in 'Interactive Learning technology improves Engineering student competencies' has spurred on the evolution of higher education from as Jansson refers "an institution that exists to provide instruction...to an institution that exists to produce learning" (p.48). Jansson's discussion is predicated by numerous papers on emerging learning theories and the impacts that professional learning have on the developments of change in higher education classrooms. Learning theories in instructional design, emerging technologies, learning styles and modalities are continuing to threaten the traditional f2f classroom where students are asked to leave their knowledge at the door and enter 19th Century style chalk and talk classrooms. As Jansson presents, "the modality through which sensory information is most effectively perceived is visual. Only about 20% of students find the verbal approaches their most effective modalities for acquiring input" (p.48).

The paradigm shift that Jansson refers has further influenced the flexible delivery mode of learning in high education. As Thomson, Tan and Brook suggest flexible delivery of higher education is a changing paradigm that is influenced by educators, students and technology. Both economic rationalism and the rapidly changing directions of technology in education have enabled students and educators with new ways of delivering content and ensuring active learning outside the traditional f2f classroom. As the contributing authors have argued, "higher education has traditionally entailed hundreds of students sitting in a lecture hall for several hours each week, spending additional time at on–campus libraries and joining an array of student organizations" (Thomson, Tan & Brook, p.62) has been re-negotiated by blended and fully online learning and teaching over the last decade. Thomson, Tan and Brook through an examination of the use of computer-mediated communication (CMC) investigated flexible delivery modes of learning, effectiveness and student satisfaction. As Thomson, Tan & Brook confer, the tutor in this case, was the expert who led the field of study and facilitated the learning space, a finding that exemplified the research for them and many other researchers in online learning and teaching. The pedagogical outcome of a blended and fully online learning space that teaches, motivates, interacts and supports students learning is imperative for student satisfaction and engagement in LMS, VLE and this instance, Skype and synchronous chat in MSN. The instructional design of these learning and teaching approaches require learners to take more of an ownership of their learning rather than taking notes passively in a lecture situation and be more able to risk take through critical thinking strategies. As argued by the Editors, these approaches to learning in higher education has however, meant that students are often required to learn to learn online simultaneously while learning to learn.

The pedagogical consideration of instructional design online is of utmost importance to the contributing authors. Supported specifically by Carmen Besanta, whose research presents an investigation into how technology can aid in driving the pedagogy through constructivist learning. The pedagogical stance taken by the Editors is that quality teaching and learning and authentic task design within a constructivist scaffolded learning space maximizes learning in the digital teaching environment (Rourke & Coleman, 2010; 2010a; 2010b). Educational research and constructivist online learning (Vygotsy, 1978; McLoughlin & Marshall, 2000; McLoughlin, 2002) techniques in scaffolding support the hypothesis that a "learner support system" (McLoughlin & Marshall, 2000, p.1) creates a climate for learning that is supportive and driven by the pedagogy not the technology. Besanta's reflective and constructivist online active learning course development further seeks to reinforce "the important role of the teacher in virtual learning, better planning and effectiveness in web-based education than 'in-the-ground' education, more time invested into virtual leaning than into traditional teaching, satisfaction with constructive technology, feedback and motivation and usefulness of (LMS) asynchronous tools and promoting communication and assistance" (p.101).

The constructivist approach to learning is a process in which students actively participate in the learning process, while both the instructor and students scaffold the student's in task-based learning. In these spaces, voyeuristic lurkers in the class watch the discussions, read the posts and learn from the interactions of others in the course. Mark Mabrito in 'Lurking and Learning' examines these lurkers, who in the f2f classroom would be avid listeners and note-takers, listening carefully to the anecdotes and discussion in the groups. "Not every type of learner in every type of situation may benefit from direct interaction" (p.114). For students who may not have the language, educational ease or the technological know how, this online environment gives them the space and time to reflect on their learning while participating in the discussion without having to participate. Mabrito's study of the vicarious nature of these students is imperative for Online educators to see the relevance and benefit of active and collaborative learning where not only the active communicators are learning. For instructional design this study is important to consider the advantage of student's many connections, exchanges, relations and contact, because "course designs that allow for opportunities for vicarious interaction may benefit not only these students, but other students in the course as well" (p.114).

Learning styles, personality traits and educational experience and background have become important for instructional course design in online teaching and learning. As students interact with the course online and make decisions about their learning they make these depending on their modes of learning. Art and design students have specific differences online when utilizing left-brain dominated LMS. Participation, innovation and creativity are inherent themes of web 2.0, alongside pedagogical aims of collaboration, communication and contribution. These learning spaces have opened new opportunities for creative and visually literate students. Marlo Ransdell in 'Continuing the Dialogue' examined the reflective writing activities and student learning styles of graduate students to "enhance critical and creative thinking in students" (p.118). The information technology (IT) revolution is in its third decade and the field of online learning and digital teaching online is continuing to be researched and published in both teaching and learning. The editors have investigated the pedagogic benefits of blogging for students in graduate student reflective writing practice and discovered similar findings, particularly that educational blogging assists students to become subject matter experts through regular scouring, filtering and posting in the asynchronous space. While increasing student interest and ownership in learning, particularly for students working in the creative industries, blogging as a reflective practice also gives students legitimate chances to participate and en-culturates them into a CoP.

CoPs are reflected in the courses students have elected to study already, with further sub-groups and tighter communities of practice within. They develop online when as Nesbit states "students have a passion to deepen their knowledge and interact with others about the topic," when "students already know each other, or are given a chance to get to know each other in person as part of the course," or when "students are from similar contexts and/or share similar experiences" (p.124). CoPs play an important role in online learning and teaching, particularly for students in an elective course who have shared knowledge and experiences that promote familiarity and secure place to study at ease. As collaborative learning inspires self directed students to risk take, critically reflect and work together as a CoP, Mobile Learning has taken the development of online learning out of the classroom and into the student's personal space. Black and Hawkes present another paradigm shift, from the student on a chair with fold out desk and pen in hand in developed countries to the image of a student with mobile learning device and net book. This, they propose will address issues in primary and secondary education particularly in the area of reading comprehension.

Learning and teaching online has provided the 21st Century teacher with new teaching possibilities to engage students in collaborative and self-directed learning experiences utilising web 2 technology. Web 2.0 implies a step change from one level to the next, which has had considerable impact on the learning of students (Coleman & Rourke, 2010). This step change "promises learners new opportunities to be independent in their study and research...encourage a wider range of expressive capability...facilitate more collaborative ways of working and...furnish a setting for learner achievements to attract an authentic audience" (Crook, Cummings, Fisher, Graber, Harrison, Lewin, Logan, Luckin, Oliver, & Sharples, 2008, p.5). The encouragement of self-direction in student learning alongside these new opportunities as Crook et al., (2008) refers, include opportunities for teachers to focus on inquiry, literacy, collaboration and publication in the social framework of web 2.0. Making collaborative learning mobile has enhanced these emerging technologies. As Black and Hawkes indicate "research illustrates that the development and implementation of this type of collaborative mobile learning application is indeed possible" (p.155).

An increase in online capabilities has led to further accessibility and an increase in learning communities, this has created a shift in collaborations from the f2f classroom to the online collaborative learning (OCL) space. This digitally enriched environment is not without its issues; digital literacy is an ever-growing field of research in education that is accompanied by text-based literacy levels on the decrease in developing countries. Collaborative learning is enhanced as mobile devices are also improved by peer review and greater student led learning cooperatives that encourage participation. Online peer review unlike f2f peer review offers students an anonymous space to share their knowledge and in the constructivist sense, act in the expert role. As Rourke and Coleman present, peer review and computer mediated peer review (CMPR) was utilized to offer collaborative learning and enquiry to students who had a wealth of experience and knowledge in the field in which their peers were researching. West contributes to the field through research into collaborative learning and writing tools. Assisting students writing in higher education can improve writing efficiency and fluency. West indicates the use of collaborative wikis can further enhance mobile learning through the use of social writing tools for learning and assessment.

Learning in the digital age ideologically bases its educational theories as stated in the work of constructivism and scaffolding for online learning and teaching. Cortina-Prerez (2006) suggested that an eLearning framework is shaped by four characteristics: "learner centredness; hypertext; authenticity, and autonomy" (p.130-131). These descriptions, aid in the argument for elearning and its potential as a transformative learning tool. These four features are indicators of best practice in both f2f and online teaching and learning. Ensuring that teaching is focused on the learner, uses hyper-textuality, is authentic and promotes autonomy is inherent in all good teaching practice. This best practice, includes a sense of community. Community in the learning space supports student's 'learning to learn online' and to learn course content. Wests' case study seeks to reflect upon students' collaborative efforts and uses and ultimately evaluates the tools available in web 2.0. West chose a wiki that was "harnessed to foster a dynamic learning culture that allows students to create, review, reflect, evaluate and modify the knowledge and outcomes of a group" (p.193). Wikis are collaborative writing tools that offer users the ability to "discuss, comment, edit, reflect, evaluate and ultimately complete a shared outcome" (p193). As with West's reflection on wikis, all contributors in this book have a shared outcome and common goal in mind, to use technology to enhance and improve student learning and teaching, not utilising 'technology for technologies sake', a worthy aim for the 21st century educator.

References

Biggs, (1999). *Teaching for quality learning at university : what the student does.* 1st Edition, Philadelphia : Society for Research into Higher Education : Open University Press.

Coleman, K. S. & Rourke, A. J. (2010). Art education 2.0: Participation, innovation and creativity in the digitised classroom, *Journal of Art Education Australia, 33, Special Edition Issue* 2,140-153.

Cortina-Pérez, B. (2006). Teaching and Learning English through WebCT Tools: Promoting Digital Scaffolding. *International Journal of Technology, Knowledge and Society* 2(5), 129-138.

Cronin, J.C., (1993). Four misconceptions about authentic learning. *Educational Leadership*, 50(70), 78-80.

Crook, C., Cummings, J., Fisher, T., Graber, R., Harrison, C., Lewin, C., Logan, K., Luckin, R., Oliver, M. & Sharples, M. (2008). *Web 2.0 Technologies for Learning: The current landscape – Opportunities, Challenges and Tensions*. BECTA, UK. http://partners.becta.org.uk/uploaddir/downloads/page_documents/research/web2_technologies_learning.pdf

Herrington, J, Reeves, T.C & Oliver, R. (2010). *A Guide to Authentic e-learning*. Routledge, New York.

Jonassen, D., (1991). Evaluating Constructivistic learning. *Educational Technology*, 31(9), 28-33.

Lancaster, L. C., & Stillman, D. (2002). *When generations collide*. New York: HarperCollins.

McLoughlin, C. (2002). Learner Support in Distance and Networked Learning Environments: Ten Dimensions for Successful Design. *Distance Education*, 23(2), 149-162.

McLoughlin, C. & Lee, M.J.W. (2009). Personalised learning spaces and self-regulated learning: Global examples of effective pedagogy. In *Same places, different spaces. Proceedings ascilite Auckland 2009.* http://www.ascilite.org.au/conferences/auckland09/procs/mcloughlin.pdf

McLoughlin, C. & Marshall, L. (2000). Scaffolding: A model for learner support in an online teaching environment. In Hermann, A. & Kulski, M.M., (Eds), *Flexible Futures in Tertiary Teaching*. Proceedings of the 9th Annual Teaching Learning Forum, NPN.

Prensky, M. (2001). Digital natives, digital immigrants Part 1. *On The Horizon, 9*(5), 1-6.

Rourke, A.J & Coleman, K.S. (2010a). A Learner Support System: Scaffolding to Enhance Digital Learning. *The International Journal of Technology, Knowledge and Society*, 6 (1) 55-70. http://www.Technology-Journal.com

Rourke, A.J & Coleman, K.S. (2010b). Knowledge building in 21st Century: learners, learning and educational practice. In C. Steel, M.J. Keppell & P. Gerbic, *Curriculum, technology & transformation for an unknown future*. Proceedings ascilite Sydney 2010.

Vygotsy, L. (1978). *Mind in Society*. Cambridge, MA: Harvard University Press.

Part I

Interactive Technologies for Learning

Lenses for Digital Inclusion

A social work framework for research, policy and practice

Deborah West

Introduction

The digital divide is best conceived of as a reflection of broader social divides which exist within society and contribute to the experience of social exclusion on many levels. The digital divide is generally referred to in relation to the use of computers and the Internet however it is useful to consider such differences as one aspect of a technological divide. This is based on the fact that information technology and micro processing has become embedded in a range of items used in daily life.

In addition, the technological revolution and associated shift to an information economy is intrinsically linked to the idea of lifelong learning. Learning across the lifespan is now seen as vital for economic, social and political inclusion in an increasingly technological society.

While research on the digital divide has expanded in recent years, it has in many ways been limited by our initial efforts at conceptualising the issue. This has led to research, policy and practice which has left a significant portion of the population further disadvantaged. This paper presents an alternative framework for understanding, researching and responding to the issue of the digital divide. It is based on social work theory and knowledge from the fields of technology and lifelong learning as well as three separate research studies.

Background

Expanding the Digital Divide Framework

Early conceptualizations of the digital divide considered only physical access to computers resulting in a binary notion of simply whether a person had access or not. Work in this area has identified the factors of income and education as key indicators of computer ownership followed by age (National Office for the Information Economy, 2000; National Telecommunications and Information Administration, 2000). These findings clearly connect digital exclusion to underlying social inequities.

In recent years the term has been broadened to include factors such as professional knowledge and the technical skills needed to make use of information and communication technologies (Kling; 1998), type of connection (Davison & Cotton, 2003), digital literacy (Koehler, 2001 in Scott, Burmeister et al., 2002), global differences (Ghahremani, 2001), location and differences in access (OECD, 2001) and content (Carvin, 2000)

DiMaggio and Hargittai (in Hargittai 2002) suggest five dimensions along where a digital divide may exist:

1. technical means (software, hardware, connection quality)
2. autonomy of use (location of access, freedom to use for own purposes)
3. use patterns (types of use of internet)
4. social support networks (availability of assistance if needed, size of networks)
5. skill (one's own ability to use medium effectively)

This framework goes much further in considering the many aspects which contribute to the digital divide and begins to focus research into some more useful areas. However, this could be expanded further and more importantly consider why some groups face a digital divide in relation to each item.

Incorporating Lifelong Learning

Lifelong learning is a concept which has gained prominence over the past 30 years (Tuijnman, 1999). The increasing urgency in the quest for lifelong learning is seen to be a result of many contemporary factors including the "widening impact of technology, globalization, trade liberalization, the ageing population, growing cultural and ethnic diversity and the changing nature of work" (OECD, 1996, p. 15).

Lifelong learning is often referred to as being "lifelong and lifewide" (OECD, 1996). "Lifelong" highlights the over-riding perspective that learning occurs throughout life and draws attention to the ongoing developmental process of all individuals (Delors, 1996). It emphasizes learning and development as occurring throughout the life course.

"Lifewide" refers to learning across a range of settings and experiences. The various settings are referred to as formal, non formal and informal. Formal education refers to institutionally based education including schools and Universities where much emphasis is placed on learning with computers. Non formal education can be defined as "any organised educational activity outside of the established formal system ... that is intended to serve identifiable learning clienteles and learning objectives" (Cropley, 1989 p.15). The many computer classes which operate often fall within this sphere.

Informal learning is defined as a "lifelong process whereby all individuals acquire attitudes, values, skills, and knowledge from daily experience and from the educative influences and resources in their environment – from family and neighbours, from work and play, from the marketplace, the library, and the mass media" (Cropley, 1989, p. 15). Informal learning is the most common form of learning yet is under-researched and often ignored.

In the current environment being able to use computers is a foundation skill for lifelong learning and is justifiably included as a basic literacy skill however it is also one goal for many people in the process of lifelong learning. For those people who do not have such skills the act of learning to use a computer is a process of learning in itself. In addition, many people who are most likely to benefit from lifelong learning are those who are currently excluded from it or lack the self confidence to embark on the process (Fryer, 1999). They are also the same people who are least likely to have access to or know how to use a computer.

Methodology

This framework was developed as a result of PhD research conducted by the author. The thesis was based on three separate studies which considered barriers for older people to the use of technology, learning preferences in computer classes and computer class design features which facilitated learning. The results of these studies contributed separately to the development of this framework (West, 2003b).

Incorporating a social work perspective, the three separate but related studies conducted considered:

1. motivations for learning about technology to identify how this may fit with life stage needs and the barriers to learning about and using technology in order to identify and highlight potential difficulties in achieving a "goodness of fit";
2. how varying learning programs may improve the transactions by increasing use of technology
3. the appropriateness of learning environments and teaching approaches for sub-groups

The data for the three studies was drawn from two separate groups in South Australia and included a total of 2345 respondents over the age of 65. Data was collected via self-completed pre and post intervention questionnaires, interviews and non-participant observation. Due to the scope of the project the specific methodology for each study will not be discussed. Such detail can be gained from a variety of independent publications which are referenced in the following discussion.

While the specific population considered in the study was older people, the framework that evolved provides a way of understanding and addressing digital disadvantage for any population group who are under-represented in the use of technology.

The Framework

This framework is made up of two levels. The first level is the application of a social work perspective to the area of the digital divide. This is based on the premise that the digital divide is a reflection of broader social inequities. Therefore to understand or address the issue one must understand the root cause of social inequity. The second level of the framework builds on and extends the existing frameworks on the digital divide.

The third column in the model shows the reflexive nature and application of the framework. The combination of the social work perspective with the use of lenses and critical consideration of factors affecting the digital divide will lead to research, programmes and policy that is clearly focused and informed to achieve the overall objective. In addition, the model is seen as spiralling to emphasise the fact that we must continually seek to understand blocks to inclusion at all levels and across the range of programmes to generate evidence based practice. As such policy, research and programme development are linked and praxis is a key outcome.

Figure 1: Framework for Inquiry into the Technological Divide

The Social Work Perspective

The key social work purpose, "to improve the transactions between people and their environments and to facilitate a better match-that is, a 'goodness of fit' between human needs and environmental resources" (Germain & Gitterman, 1986 p. 630), is at the heart of the framework. This focus on the person-in-environment draws attention to the importance of the political, social and cultural milieus in shaping the overall development, opportunities and experiences of each person. As related to the current research this is seen as the fit between the individual and the increasingly technological society.

The social work perspective is used as the theoretical foundation for the research and as a key component of the framework. The Empowerment Model of Social Work Practice as developed by Judith Lee (1994) was seen as particularly relevant in considering the area of digital disadvantage. Lee's work has at its core the empowerment of disadvantaged groups in society.

Due to the pervasiveness of the problem of the current mismatch between the individual and the technological environment, overcoming the digital divide is best considered in light of the process of empowerment with the goal of raising critical consciousness and translating "private troubles into public issues" (Schwartz: 1969). Applied to our area of study this means that knowledge about and use of technology is associated with power and that blocks to power are imposed and compound to create further disadvantage. This highlights the fact that the technological playing field is not even and some population groups are more likely to be disadvantaged under the current structure.

Lee's (1994) model, which draws upon and synthesizes a range of models and prior thinking, advocates the use of "fifocal vision" to understand the relative position of individuals and groups. The five factors considered to be at the core of the individual's experience in society are seen as "lenses" through which all interactions should be viewed. This provides a way of critically looking at the place of the individual or population group in the broader social structure and how that impacts on all opportunities including digital inclusion.

1. History of Oppression

History can be viewed from many perspectives but for the purpose of this discussion it seems prudent to consider two areas from where oppression may arise – the historical placement of the individual in the society and the historical trends that are evident in the theoretical and analytical discussion of any population group.

2. Ecological View

An ecological view acknowledges the human experience of development throughout the life course. The ecological view includes knowledge on stress and coping, adaptation, ego functioning and cognition. An understanding of the impact of life cycle changes is particularly important when considering population groups who are disadvantaged in relation to technology such as older people.

3. Ethclass Perspective

An ethclass perspective refers to "the social participation and identity of persons who are confined in their own class and ethnic group due to oppression" Gordon (1978 in Lee 1994 p.162). Adopting such a perspective will highlight the relative position of sub-populations within the society and the limits that this imposes on their participation. Important in this discussion are the ideas of social inclusion and the limitations imposed by a dominant culture on those who are different.

Social exclusion refers to the situation where individuals or communities are unable to participate in economic, social and political dimensions of society (Zappala et al., 2000). This is usually involuntary with population segments being at increased risk. Increasingly this concept is being linked to changes in the economic structure with moves to globalization and an information economy.

4. Class Structure

Lee (1994) advocates that one needs to consider the class structure of the society which influences the context of the individual. At its core, the structure of society is changing. Giddens (1984 p.17) states that "Structure [sic] refers, in social analysis, to the structuring properties allowing the 'binding' of time-space in social systems, the properties which make it possible for discerning similar social practices to exist across varying spans of time and space and which lend them 'systemic form'". Given this definition it can be seen that the properties which relate to the binding of time and space are indeed much different in our increasingly technological society. Online services, communication venues, communities are transforming the space aspect into that of a virtual element. The idea of time is also different with access being twenty-four hours and instantaneous.

Structure in this context is said to refer to both the resources and the rules of interaction which can be both enabling and constraining (Giddens, 1984 p.23). In our context the rules and the resources are changing dramatically. Resources are increasingly being focussed on the technological aspect of society including access, infrastructure, development of online services etc. The rules for interaction are becoming much more focussed on the virtual world with institutions and organisations directly and indirectly moving people toward this medium. If one is fully aware of the rules for engaging in the broader society it can be enabling with faster, more accessible services available. However, for those who are unaware or unable to come to terms with such rules a level of social exclusion exists from the outset. The duality of structure is important and attention must be paid to both sides of the equation thus supporting the person in environment paradigm.

Those who have control of such resources and rules hold the power in the current society and are able to manipulate the developing nature of the experience. Giddens (1984) states that "... in many contexts of social life there occur processes of selective 'information filtering' whereby strategically placed actors seek reflexively to regulate the overall conditions of system reproduction either to keep things as they are or to change them." (pp.27-28) Drawing on the work of Marx and Weber, the political economy perspective considers the importance of economic factors in social stratification but also considers how socio-cultural factors are relevant to the distribution of material and symbolic benefits (Quadagno, 1999).

5. Feminist Perspective

The use of a feminist perspective calls attention to the personal as political, gender differences and power imbalances. The feminist perspective of the personal as political fits with the person-in-environment framework, a core element of social work practice. In doing so it calls attention to the structural level which impacts on the individual and is particularly relevant in the context of our current technological society. This highlights the domination of systems which subsequently impact on inequalities in the use of technology by age, gender, race and ethnicity. Of particular importance are the power imbalances inherent in the accumulation of and access to the skills to gain that knowledge.

In considering the concept of power Hartman (1992 in Valentich, 1996) drawing on the work of Foucault makes the case that power and knowledge are one. This has significant implications in terms of the use of technology and knowledge about how to use such technology. With the move to a knowledge or information society, knowledge is frequently held in electronic form and therefore the ability to access such knowledge relies on computer based skills. A feminist perspective calls attention to the implications for a lower level of use of technology by different demographic population and women in particular.

Applying the concept of gender raises some key issues as technology is generally described as male and the field of technology is predominated by men (Barnett et al., 2000) which therefore impacts on its design, content and use. Barnett et al. (2000) make the case that the male bias in the field of technology means that a male bias is inherent in the design of technology which results in computers being more accessible to males.

Feminine perspectives suggest that women have different ways of knowing which lead to differences in learning styles. Therefore classes on technology which are designed to suit the broader population are more likely to be taught by men and incorporate a masculine orientation to learning raising issues in terms of the suitability of classes for any female.

The Technological Divide

The second level of the framework highlights the factors that are more specific to unequal access and use of technology. While this includes some of the factors that have previously been included in digital divide frameworks, it goes further to draw attention to the multiple underpinnings of these. It provides a structure to consider more fully the factors that impact on variations in the use and applications of technology. These factors were identified through the study on the barriers to the use of technology (West, 2003a; 2003b).

1. Access

The category of access must be broken down to include both technical means and autonomy of use.

a. Technical Means

This category incorporates those items which have been previously viewed as the heart of the digital divide including variations in access to technology based on the availability of hardware, software and supporting infrastructure. It is necessary to move beyond simply the cost of the equipment as a major barrier to include investigation of the quality of connection to the Internet, the design barriers in technology and the availability of appropriate equipment.

In relation to the quality of connection, not all lines are equal. There is great variation in the options that are available as well as the reliability and flexibility of the both the telecommunication infrastructure and service provision for Internet connection.

Even where basic services are available and adequate, the design of the hardware and software poses significant barriers for large segments of the community. The findings of Study One (West, 2003a; West, 2003b) indicated that significant structural barriers existed and suggest that investigation is required into the appropriateness of hardware and software design for a range of user groups beyond what has been considered to date.

Where the equipment does pose barriers a range of options may be available to increase the ease of use for many people. Consideration needs to be given to the availability of and access to such accessibility features and again cost, quality and knowledge play key roles.

b. Autonomy of Use

The location of access is a key element in whether someone will actually use equipment. Factors to consider are the actual location of access whether it be at home, work, school, a friend or relative's house, or a public access point.

The appropriateness of the location in relation to the individual is also important. A location which is not conducive to concentration or provides little opportunity for privacy is likely to have an impact on the frequency as well as the type of applications that are utilized (Irizarry et al., 2002; 2001). For example, a public access point in a community centre may be noisy and lack privacy, and therefore not seen as a good place to research something of a private nature or do one's banking.

A related issue is the freedom to use the equipment for one's own purposes. Access at work is likely to place restrictions on the use of the Internet for personal interests or private concerns. Similar issues may exist for a range of other types of technology where funding arrangements or service providers limit the availability of equipment for particular groups or for particular purposes.

2. Knowledge and Awareness

Knowledge of the range of equipment that is available, the application of the technology, the range of modifications that are available is vital in order for people to make an informed decision about whether or not to pursue its use. People may not be aware of the range of applications or the fit with their own needs and goals or how equipment may be appropriately modified. This factor links back to motivation to engage in learning about technology as it is connected to the idea of relevance (West, 2003a; 2003b). Knowledge and awareness of the variety and broad application of technology allows individuals to make their own connections to relevant goals and needs. This is a key first step in the process of engaging in the learning process. Over-riding this element of the digital divide is the idea that knowledge is power and knowledge and awareness of technology is more likely to lead to the individual being able to make an informed choice about the pursuit and application of the technology.

3. Learning Opportunities and Support

The inclusion of this category in any analysis of the digital divide is seen as imperative for several reasons. First, there is great variation in the opportunities for learning and the amount of support that is available on an ongoing basis. Second, and perhaps more significantly, it formalizes the links between the concept of lifelong learning and the digital divide. Lifelong learning, as discussed, has implicit links to the use of information and communication technology, and acknowledging such links in discussions on the digital divide begins to operationalise the concept. Initial areas requiring consideration are:

a. Formal and non formal learning

In terms of learning opportunities and support, consideration needs to be given to the factors which impact on participation in formal and non formal learning environments. A range of classes should be offered to suit the different skill levels and interests across populations. For example the provision of classes about general technology may serve as an entry point for many individuals who do not have a specific interest in computers and may help them to become familiar with the principles behind technology or make decisions about the usefulness of such technology to them (Irizarry, Downing & West, year). In addition, classes may increase their confidence and pique their interest to pursue further learning around computers and technology (West, 2002). Increased confidence in relation to general technology lays the foundation for the potential to use technology should the need arise in the future, as in the case of health or safety items (West, 2002).

For those who choose to enter a computer class, learning preferences and styles will vary. Mainstream classes are unlikely to meet the learning needs of many target groups and will result in the only the "easy targets" being reached. Study Three investigated such preferences as well as the link between the design features and the increased use of technology. The results indicated that particular factors have a significant impact on different demographic segments (West, 2003b). There is a need for further investigation into the optimal design features for a range of other target groups.

The basic factors of cost, location, timing and access are all seen as having a major impact on the individual's engagement in any learning activity, particularly in relation to rural and remote areas where appropriate classes are less likely to be available.

The idea of design barriers should also be addressed through the inclusion of awareness raising as well as opportunities to try equipment which incorporates universal design or accessibility features. Due to the fact that such design features are seen as a major barrier to the use of technology, this inclusion in classes serves several purposes. It increases awareness of available options, gives people a chance to try and become familiar with such items in a supported environment and perhaps more importantly acknowledges difficulties in using equipment as a structural issue. This has the effect of normalizing and reframing the experience of the individual and will help to increase self esteem and confidence.

b. informal

Investigating frustration and satisfaction levels in relation to technology in Study Two indicated that these factors were impacted on by something external to the class (West, 2003b). It was subsequently proposed that one such external factor may be informal learning. The impact of such informal learning is an area which requires much attention as little has been given. The range, quality, applicability and impact of informal learning opportunities requires further investigation.

The idea of having technical and proficient support at home and the availability of that support were listed as a factor in Study One (West, 2003a; 2003b). Many people indicated that they fear when problems go wrong as they have no one available to help them or that they feel uncomfortable asking for such help. The size of one's social support networks is likely to have an impact on the availability of such specific support and cross-generational contact may be a significant factor in the case of older people. The idea of having support at home also offers vast potential in the area of informal learning.

4. Skill

a. Technical Skill

The level of skill of the individual is likely to vary considerably with some people demonstrating that they can only manage the basics while others appear much more advanced. Skill will impact on the actual use of technology as well as the time taken to complete tasks, the support required to complete tasks, confidence to undertake training, the appropriateness of access points etc. It is also likely to be an indicator and reflection of the variation in applications and frequency of use. Whether someone has access to or uses a computer is in not reflective of their skill level.

b. Literacy, Language, Content and Information Literacy

Basic literacy is vital to participate in the use of technology and it is possible that variation in literacy levels is one factor in the lower level of use by people with lower educational attainment. The barrier imposed by language for people from a non-English speaking background is a related factor. The issue of literacy is complicated by use of more technical and unfamiliar language than in previous periods of history.

Understanding the language being used in today's society is vital to social inclusion, bridging generation gaps as well as being able to purchase equipment and navigate instructions. The use of technical language was found to be a key barrier in Study One (West, 2003b). Motivation to learn about technology was found to be partially associated with overcoming language barriers in order to bridge gaps with one's children and grandchildren, keep up with technology and communicate with trade people (West, 2003b). The potential for escalating technological development would suggest that the issue of unfamiliar language may be with us for a very long time.

Information Literacy relates to the idea that one is able to efficiently access required information and be able to make sound judgements on the quality and relevance of content. This means knowing how to perform searches and having enough initial knowledge to be able to enter key words. The task then becomes one of sorting through websites and making judgements about whether it is relevant and reliable information. Being able to manage this process is vital to avoid becoming overwhelmed by the amount of information available.

Content in relation to the World Wide Web is a major issue which is largely neglected. The vast majority of internet sites are English based or based on an English entry point and the relevance of such sites to many people is limited. In addition, the appropriateness of content is also linked to the idea of information literacy.

c. Use patterns

There is great variation in the use of computers and technology. What is often reported is whether a) an individual has access to a computer and b) uses a computer or not. This does not produce an accurate picture of variations in use or variation according to frequency and application especially since access does not necessarily translate to use. A computer may be present in a home however only one member of the household may use it. For example, a figure often quoted is that 68% of Australian households have computer and 62% have internet access (DCITA, 2005) yet this may mean that only one or two people in the house use it regularly. With the figures on home computer ownership much higher for families with children, it may be that the children use the computer frequently but the adults use it rarely.

Application is also an important consideration. Some people only use their computer to type letters or for email but others may email, shop, bank and gather information using the Internet. In relation to other types of technology, a good example is that of a bank access card. The different levels of use was highlighted by Rogers and Cabrera (1996) who found that many more people had an Automatic Teller Machine card than actually used it. The same may be applied to a mobile phone that one doesn't take with them or an installed watering system that is not utilized.

Particularly significant in discussions of variation in the application of information and communication technology is the link to dialogues on lifelong learning. The use of information and communication technology to access information, knowledge and a range of learning opportunities underpin all such dialogue. Learning with computers is gaining in prominence and resulting in learning around a variety of topics relying on the use of computers. The inability to use such technology is therefore likely to negatively affect the pursuit of such learning.

A connected and over-riding issue is that of full participation in society and social inclusion. As society, knowledge and information becomes more technologically based, awareness and ability to use information and communication technology to pursue interests, learning and participation in political processes will have an impact on the relative status and position of the individual within society. The thesis findings highlighted the link between power and knowledge suggesting the vital need to address varying skill levels which will impact on social inclusion. The framework discussed here emphasises the importance of the relationship between lifelong learning, technology and social inclusion in a way which is meaningful and can be addressed through research, policy and programming.

Conclusion

Digital divide frameworks have in the past been focused on some of the factors that impact on computer use. While these have expanded in recent years to better reflect the range of barriers, they need to be expanded to include other barriers and critical factors that affect digital inclusion, to acknowledge the underlying social inequities of which the digital divide is one reflection of and provide a framework to develop appropriate programmes and policies that will facilitate digital inclusion. Without such a framework, we will continue to reach only the "easy targets", that is those people most likely to overcome the barriers.

The driving force behind the framework is a social work approach based on the principles of social justice and empowerment. At the individual level, mastering technology, a positive learning experience and feeling a part of society all contribute to increased self esteem and a feeling of control over one's environment. At a structural level the use of technology is becoming increasingly necessary in today's society and learning how to use such technology is considered to be a vital element in the process of social inclusion.

The framework presented in this paper is comprised of two key elements: the lenses by which to understand broader social inequities and a digital divide framework based on an empirical study on the barriers to use of technology. The framework is seen as a tool for guiding research on the digital divide to identify and refine policy directions and programmes as part of a dynamic process of critical reflection that guides practice.

References

Barnett, K.R., Buys, L.R. and Adkins, B. (2000) "Information and Communication Practices: the Joint Concerns of Age and Gender in the Information Age." *Australasian Journal on Ageing*, 19(2): 69-74.

Carvin, A. (2000) "Mind the Gap: The Digital Divide as the Civil Rights Issue of the New Millennium." MulitMedia Schools, January/February http://infotoday.com/MMSchools/Jan00/carvin.htm

Davison, E. & Cotton, S.R. (2003) "Connection Discrepancies: Unmasking further layers of the digital divide." *First Monday*, 8(3). http://www.firstmonday.org/issues/issue8_3/davison

Cropley, A.J. (1989) "Lifelong Education: Interaction with Adult Education"in C.J. Titmus (ed) *Lifelong Education for Adults: An International Handbook*. pp. 145-146. Pergamon Press, Sydney.

Delors, J. (1996) *Learning: The Treasure Within*. United Nations Educational, Scientific and Cultural Organisation, Paris.

Department of Communications, Information Technology and the Arts (2005) *The Current State of Play*. Australian Government, Canberra.

Fryer, R.H. (1999) *Creating Learning Cultures: Next Steps in Achieving the Learning Age*. National Advisory Group for Continuing Education and Lifelong Learning, London. http://www.lifelonglearning.co.uk/nagcell/index.htm

Germain, C.B. & Gitterman, A. (1986) "The Life Model Approach to Social Work Revisited" in F.J. Turner (ed) *Social Work Treatment: Interlocking Theoretical Approaches*. pp. 618-644. The Free Press, New York.

Ghahremani, Y. (2001) "Heroes of the Digital Divide" *Asia Week*. June http://www.asiaweek.com/asiaweek/technology/article/0,8707,132165,00.html

Giddens, A. (1984) *The Constitution of Society: Outline of the Theory of Structuration.* Polity Press, Cambridge.

Hargittai, E. (2002) "Second-Level Digital Divide: Differences in People's Online Skills" *First Monday* 7(4): http://firstmonday.org/issues/issue7_4/hargittai/index.html

Irizarry, C., Downing A., West. D. (2002) "Promoting Modern Technology and Internet Access for Under-Represented Populations", *Journal of Technology in Human Services,* 19(4) pp. 13-30

Irizarry, C., West, D., Downing A. (2001) "Use of the internet by older rural South Australians", *Australasian Journal on Ageing*, 20(3), pp. 153-155.

Kling, R. (1998) *Technological and Social Access on Computing, Information and Communication Technologies.* White Paper for Presidential Advisory Committee on High Performance Computing and Communications, Information Technology and the Next Generation Internet. Washington, DC. http://www.slis.indiani.edu/kling/pubs/NGI.htm

Lee, J.A.B. (1994) *The Empowerment Approach to Social Work Practice*. Columbia University Press, New York.

National Office for the Information Economy (2002) *The Digital Divide*, Australian Government, Canberra.

National Telecommunications and Information Administration, Economics and Statistics Administration (2000) *Falling Through the Net: Toward Digital Inclusion: A report on American's Access to Technology Tools*. US Department of Commerce, Washington, DC. http://www.ntia.doc.gov/ntiahome/digitaldivide

Organisation for Economic Cooperation and Development: Directorate for Science, Technology and Industry (2001) *Understanding the Digital Divide*. OECD, Paris. http://www.oecd.org

Organisation for Economic Cooperation and Development (1996) *Lifelong Learning for All*. OECD, Paris.

Quadagno, J. and Reid, J. (1999) "The Political Economy Perspective in Aging." In V.L. Bengston and K.W. Schaie (eds) *Handbook of Theories of Aging*. pp. 344-358. Springer Publishing Company, New York.

Rogers, W., Cabrera, E., Walker, N. and Fisk, D. (1996) "Training Older Adults to Use Automatic Teller Machines" *Human Factors*, 38(3): 425-433

Schwartz, W. (1969) "Private Troubles and Public Issues: One Social Work Job or Two." In P. Weinberger (ed) *Perspectives on Social Welfare: An Introductory Anthology*. Macmillan Publishing, New York.

Scott, H., Burmeister, O.K. and Roberts, S. (2002) "Accessible E-Commerce: Crossing the digital generation gap." Third International Conference of the Australian Institute of Computer Ethics, 30 September, Australia. http://www.cota.org.au/aice.htm

Tuijnman, A. (1999) "Research Agenda for lifelong learning: a report by the Task Force of the International Academy of Education." In A. Tuinjman and T. Schuller (eds) *Lifelong Learning Policy and Research*. pp. 1-22. Portland Press, London.

Valentich, M. (1996) "Feminist Theory and Social Work Practice." In F.J. Turner (ed) *Social Work Treatment: Interlocking Theoretical Approaches*. pp. 282-318. The Free Press, New York.

West, D. (2003a) "Is Computer Access Enough: A Multilevel Analysis of the Barriers to Engagement", *Southern Review: Communication, Politics and Culture, Special Issue: Wired Communities: Information Policy at the Local and Regional Level*, 36(1).

West, D. (2003b) *Bridging the Gap: Facilitating Older People's Participation in the Use of Technology*. PhD Thesis, The Flinders University of South Australia, Adelaide.

West, D. (2002) "Engaging the Non-User of Information Technology: Barriers and Motivations" published in the refereed proceedings of the 5th *Community Networking Conference: Electronic Networking 2002- Building Community*, Melbourne, 3-5 July.

Zappala, G., Green, V. and Parker, B. (2000) *Social Exclusion and disadvantage in the New Economy*. Working Paper No. 2.20., The Smith Family, Research and Advocacy Team, Sydney.

Online Bounded Learning Community Using Universal Design and Adult Learning

Linda E. Robinson, Robert D. Hannafin and David R. Parker

Introduction

In higher education, the social nature of learning is no longer limited to in-person interactions. Technology provides new interaction options that change the very nature of the learning environment (Harasim, Hiltz, Teles, & Turoff, 1995). According to the Sloan Corporation's (2005) annual survey on online education, the number of students taking at least one online course in the U.S. as of Fall 2004 is over 2 million, and that number has surely grown since then. Additionally, many university programs blend distance technologies with traditional classrooms (Holmes, Polhemus, & Jennings, 2005). Blended learning combines instruction from two historically separate models of teaching and learning: traditional face-to-face instruction with computer-mediated instruction (Bonk & Graham, 2005). Researchers have investigated topics such as how online course participants establish identity, social presence, and community (Haythornthwaite, Kazmer, Robins, & Shoemaker, 2000; Rovai, 2001), produce coherent online discussions (Herring, 1999; Lapadat, 2002), and support adult learning principles (Whittle, Morgan, & Maltby, 2000). Researchers have found that online discourse can support critical reflection (Bonk, Hixon, & Yamagata-Lynch, 2002; Lapadat, 2002) and blended online learning is particularly effective in facilitating reflective practices (Garrison & Kanuka, 2004).

The Problem

Preservice teachers have historically expressed only limited satisfaction with many of the large lecture-style required ("core") courses in many of the teacher preparation programs around the country. Northeast University (NEU), a large public university in New England, tried to redesign one such course, a special education course required of all pre-service teachers. Faculty teach core courses in the pre-service program at NEU in large classrooms with over 100 students, making it difficult to find time for meaningful classroom discussion, to apply concepts to personal classroom situations, or for peer-to-peer interactions among students. Coupled with the challenge of large student numbers, NEU faculty confronted a need to find a way to better infuse technology into the course. The instructional team determined that the best alternative was to design the course as a blended class using both face-to-face and online learning, thus allowing the instructors to handle the large class size while creating a climate for discussion and individualized learning.

Although online learning holds promise for promoting critical discourse and challenging students' existing mental models, for some adults the risks perceived with these interactions are too great for them to participate effectively. As early as 1974, More reported that high levels of anxiety and perceived risk can cause adults to drop out of online courses. The high attrition rate in online courses (Carr, 2000; Diaz, 2002) may be a reflection of this aversion. For instance, Gutierrez (1982) suggested that low risk-takers are less willing to experience social embarrassment when making verbal contributions in face-to-face classes. The same likely holds true in online environments, in which courses that require participants to share in public forums (e.g., threaded discussions, chat rooms, and posting of work), place adults with an aversion to social sharing at a distinct disadvantage.

The problem for this study became the need to develop a blended course that supported learners to take risks in their learning. In designing activities and the learning environments, the instructors (authors) relied upon their expertise in the areas of Adult Learning theories (AL) and Universal Design for Instruction (UDI) © to build a social learning environment that facilitated a community of practice, using technology to enhance students' learning and satisfaction with the course.

Theoretical Framework

The authors drew from their own experiences and practices. One instructor was expert in Adult Learning (AL) and was able to emphasize strategies that met the needs of these young adults. Adult Learning theory actually encompasses a variety of theories that identify characteristics of adult learners and how best to meet their learning needs. The lead instructor for the course looked to the principles Universal Design for Instruction (UDI) for guidance. As society has become more appreciative of human diversity, architects and engineers learned to incorporate universal design principles when designing buildings or manufactured products, with features such as curb cuts and automatic door openers becoming common examples of design features that were immediately accessible to a wide range of individuals. Researchers in higher education have recently adapted UD principles to instructional environments. Scott, McGuire, and Shaw (2003) defined Universal Design for Instruction (UDI) as an approach to teaching that benefits a broad range of learners including students with disabilities. The nine Principles of UDI provide a design framework to enable faculty to be proactively meet many needs of increasingly diverse student learners.

The use of AL and UDI Principles initially guided the pedagogical practices and development of course activities in a "blended" instructional design. Both AL and UDI principles address the benefits of developing *communities of practice* (CoPs; Lave & Wenger, 1991). CoPs develop as informal, self-organized networks of people in areas of practice or profession. A CoP (Lave & Wenger, 1991) refers to the process of social learning that occurs when people who have a common interest in some subject or problem informally collaborate over an extended period to share ideas, find solutions, and build innovations. Brown and Duguid (1991) studied Xerox repair representatives who attempted to follow the company manuals and course training to repair complex systems but too often found the official manuals inadequate. The study revealed that successful representatives became experts from in-lunchroom conversations and other "social" occasions via the exchange of "war stories" about ways to fix certain machine problems that had no solutions in the official repair manuals. They also shared valuable stories about how to deal with difficult customers, an important topic not included in their formal training. Brown and Duguid called this informal type of work-related social grouping a "community of practice." However, based on most traditional definitions of CoPs, the authors determined that such a social learning group did not fit within the constraints of formal coursework.

Wilson, Ludwig-Hardman, Thornam, and Dunlap (2004) suggested a new type of CoP, one that was formally created by expectations of participation and bounded by the timeframe of a typical online course. These Bounded Learning Communities (BLCs) develop in direct response to guidance provided by instructors and supervisors, supported by a cumulative resource base. These and other researchers (Kreijnsa, Kirschnerb, & Jochemsb, 2003) suggest that an online atmosphere of trust and safety must exist before individuals share and articulate newly constructed knowledge. BLCs offer this. Although some adults willingly engage in the social interactions of learning, others may be reluctant to enter into unfamiliar settings (Rehn, 1990). There are seven features (Wilson et al., 2004) that seem to facilitate the creation of BLCs: shared goals, safe and supportive conditions, collective identify, collaboration, respectful inclusion, progressive discourse toward knowledge building, and mutual appropriation. In using these features, the focus of the course design became to facilitate the emergence of a BLC while exploring connections between AL, UDI and BLCs (Table 1). The authors then analyzed data collected during the course to explore if a course designed along AL and UDI principles facilitated the emergence of a BLC.

Research Methods

According to Snow and Farr (1987), sound learning theories require a whole-person approach; otherwise learning differences will be ambiguous and isolated. Therefore, the research design for this descriptive study involved a mixed-methods investigation of academic risk-taking situated where it occurs. The authors used a concurrent triangulation strategy for collecting data, which offers comprehensive investigation with equal priority given to both qualitative and quantitative data collection. This strategy allows for convergence of the information during data interpretation, thereby corroborating findings within a single study (Greene, Caracelli, & Graham, 1989).

As noted, the setting for this study was a core course offered at NEU This course is a requirement of the pre-service teacher cohort in the spring semester. This blended course provides all pre-service teachers with an overview of the legal context and collaborative instructional skills teachers need to support the inclusive education of students with exceptional learning needs (ELN). The sample population consists of junior and a few senior students in the pre-service teacher program who were enrolled in the class EPSY 207—Exceptionality. This semester-long course has about 120 participants. The researchers did not exclude any students from the study.

Course Design

In this blended 2-credit course, students met face-to-face on a weekly basis as a large group for 1 hour 40 minutes. The instructoral team divided students into smaller online teams of approximately nine students each. Eight assignments during the 15-week semester, accounting for 75% of the class grade, required students to collaborate in between lectures. Each team received a separate case study focusing on a hypothetical student with exceptional learning needs (e.g., Attention Deficit/Hyperactivity Disorder, cerebral palsy, Gifted and Talented). Teams consisted of students from different concentration areas such as social studies education, elementary education, and music education to expose them to the diversity that characterizes actual school-based planning teams. All teams included at least one student majoring in special education. Students were to organize their groups as an Individualized Educational Planning (IEP) team and immerse themselves in an extended role-play as they developed their case across the semester. Students chose roles for themselves that reflected actual participants who might realistically serve on the hypothetical student's IEP team, such as the school principal, parent, student (depending on age), school psychologist, Special Education teacher, and regular education teacher, among others.

The lead instructor provided teams with five different prompts throughout the semester (e.g., "Using formal and informal assessment data, determine the top academic need and top non-academic need that should be the focus of this student's IEP."). Teams then discussed the prompt in person and online with consideration of course materials, outside sources such as notes from related courses and Internet resources, and observations from their school practicum experiences. Analysis of the student usage data from WebCT, the course management system (CMS), confirmed that 100% of students participated in online discussions and that 98% contributed original content to the threaded discussion for at least one prompt. Each team then posted a 2-3 page summary of their discussion and decisions in response to the prompt. As a culminating activity, each case study team created an IEP for their student using the state-approved form and decisions made about the student in the earlier team summaries. Five percent of a student's final grade reflected the average of scores anonymously provided by all other team members, rating that student's collaborative participation as a team member. During the last class session, when course evaluations were completed, students rated their team members via a paper and pencil evaluation form.

The instructional team posted assignment rubrics and weekly PowerPoint slides to the CMS website. In addition to "public" spaces that all students could access on the website, each team had its own section for posting case study discussions, drafts, and completed assignments. While students were not required to make a specified number or type of posts, they were repeatedly encouraged to exchange questions, resources, drafts, and feedback there so that the instructional team could offer comments, support, and timely feedback. With permission, the instructor posted exemplars of various teams' work samples throughout the semester after highlighting these examples in class. The table below (Table 1) indicates specific design decisions the authors made to align this class with Adult Learning and Universal Design of Instruction principles while being mindful of BLC features. Following the first year, the course design underwent minor revision, but followed the same format.

Table 1: Course Connections to BLC Features

UDI Principles	*UDI Definitions*	*Adult Learning Concepts*	*Applied Course Components*	*BLC Features*
Principle 1 Equitable use	Instruction is designed to be useful to and accessible by people with diverse abilities. Provide the same means of use for all students; identical whenever possible, equivalent when not.	Adults are relevancy-oriented and applied in their learning needs (Knowles, 1978, 1990)	▪ Use of case studies and "how-to", information directly applicable tocurrent placements. ▪ Real-world connections made to course content. ▪ Role playing and rotation of leadership roles.	**Shared Goals** **Collective Identity**
Principle 2 Flexibility in use	Instruction is designed to accommodate a wide range of individual abilities. Provide choice in methods of use.	Adults are autonomous and self-directed learners (Candy, 1991; Knowles, 1978, 1990). Adults have many barriers to their learning and are motivated differently (Merriam & Caffarella, 2007).	▪ Choices offered in student's approach to completing tasks/ projects. ▪ Information presented in a wide variety of formats. ▪ Course delivery uses a consistent approach, clear goals, and outcomes for all.	**Progressive Discourse Toward Knowledge Building**

Principle 5 Tolerance for error	Instruction anticipates variation in individual student learning pace and prerequisite skills.	Adults accumulate varied life experiences and knowledge that enhance learning (Kolb, 1984)	▪ Creativity and unique approach allowed and encouraged in completing assignments. ▪ Support provided to scaffold students with a variety of skill sets and background knowledge.	**Respectful Inclusion**
Principle 8 A community of learners	The instructional environment promotes interaction and communication among students and between students and faculty.	Adult learning involves critical reflection (Brookfield, 1986; Mezirow, 1991) Adult learning is a social process (Jarvis, 1987)	▪ Promotion of discussion and facilitation of small groups into communities of practice. ▪ Reflective practice is encouraged and modeled.	**Mutual Appropriation** **Collaboration**
Principle 9 Instructional climate	Instruction is designed to be welcoming and inclusive. High expectations are espoused for all students.	Adults are motivated and engaged for many reasons (Cross, 1981)	▪ Constructive/ timely feedback provided. ▪ Affirming environment and modeling of desired behaviors by instructor.	**Safe and Supportive Conditions**

Data Collection

Wilson et al (2004) offered a short and informal method of assessing the level of community that existed in a BLC, which the authors modified in Table 2. We used both thematic coding based on the concepts presented in this assessment framework as well as open coding to determine if a BLC existed in this course.

Table 2: Measuring a Sense of Community for BLCs

Components of a BLC	*Descriptors Used to Define the Extremes of a BLC Component*
Shared Goals	Students in this class focus on certain goals we have in common. -- to -- Projects and activities give us nothing to work together that is worthwhile.
Safe and Supportive Conditions	People feel comfortable expressing their thoughts and ideas. -- to -- I would not take too many risks in this class; not a safe environment.
Collective Identity	We enjoy a sense of connection. -- to -- I do not feel like I belong in this class.
Collaboration	We interact and work together a lot in this class. -- to -- There is not much student-to-student contact in this class.
Respectful Inclusion	We respect differences between people. -- to -- Not much effort was made to help everyone fit in.
Progressive Discourse toward Knowledge Building	Our questions and discussions help us build knowledge together. -- to -- I am working on projects to learn for myself.
Mutual Appropriation	We teach each other a lot in this class, not just relying on the teacher. -- to -- I due what is required for the group.

The authors believed that, although the BLC assessment used by Wilson et al (2004) was a useful tool, the key to the emergence of a BLC is the cultivation of a "Safe and Supportive Environment." Therefore, in addition to analysis of the online discourse to detect the existence of a BLC, we used the WebCT management system to generate a class activity overview and exported data to Excel to calculate basic class statistics. Student online discourse was analyzed (n = 118) to assess student perceptions of the risk inherent in the online course environment. We hypothesized that, if students took risks in their learning by posting comments via the CMS, they would only do so if they believed that the course environment was safe and supportive. We developed a rubric (see Table 3) to evaluate this belief, based on a review of the literature that supported five indicators for risk-taking in various domains: (a) Innovations (Spitzer, 1975), (b) Acknowledgement of Uncertainty (Lundeberg & Moch, 1995; Ponticell, 2003), (c) Questioning or Disagreement (Weber, Blais, & Betz, 2002), (d) Making Choices, and (e) Frequency of Posts. Specific supports within the literature for the indicators used in the rubric were as follows:

Evidence of Innovations (Spitzer, 1975) —"Researchers have found extremely strong positive correlations between risk-taking and innovativeness (p. 171)."

Acknowledgment of Uncertainty (Lundeberg & Moch, 1995) —"Mistakes were expected and not treated punitively, and students were encouraged to take risks and to acknowledge uncertainty (p. 322)."

Disagreement or Divergence (Weber, 2002) -- They completed a paper-and-pencil questionnaire in groups of 50–70 individuals. The questionnaire consisted of a total of 101 items in five domains of risk: financial, health/safety, recreational, ethics, and social. These domains were identified based on a review of the literature on risk-taking behaviors (p. 268)." Social activities on this scale included arguing, disagreeing, and being unconventional.

Making Choices (Clifford, 1991)—"Theories of risk taking evolved from decision-making theories, which generally postulate that people assess the probability and value of alternative action-outcomes before deciding how to behave."

Table 3: Online Discussion Rubric

Indicators of Academic Risk-Taking	**0 No Answer**	**1 Low Risk-taker**	**2 Medium Risk-taker**	**3 High Risk-taker**
Evidence of Innovations		Offers no creative or innovative suggestions.	Builds upon innovations or suggestions of others	Initiates new approaches or solutions. Shows confidence in suggestions
Acknowledgement of Uncertainty		Asks simple or informational questions	Asks higher order questions and/or admits confusion	Asks subjective and/or reflective questions and suggests or admits to lack of understanding
Disagreement or Divergence		Does not disagree, follows the lead of others	Disagrees on factual or declarative information	Disagrees on subjective or reflective topics and offers personal beliefs or interpretations as support
Making Choices		Does not make a choice, but may acknowledge that a decision is needed by others	Makes a choice without revealing personal beliefs/ thoughts	Makes a choice and offers personal reflections or insights about the decision
Posts Frequency		0 to 2	3 to 6	7 or More
Total Score				
When using the Academic Risk Taking Scale, Low Risk Takers = 1 and High Risk Takers = 15.				

Rubric scores could range from 0 to 15, with a single trained researcher reading all posts for a student and assigning them a score from 1 to 3 for each of the five indicators of risk, with student posts read and scored twice to check for consistency and reliability of the rubric. It should be noted that lack of a second scoring should be considered a small limitation of this research process. If scores were inconsistent, another researcher scored them. Indicator totals were added together to obtain a risk score for each student. Scores ranged from 4 to 15. The students were grouped by total scores into low (4 to 7), medium (8 to 12) and high (13 to 15) risk groups.

Results and/or Conclusion

There were 118 students (26 males, 92 females) in the class. Table 4 provides a summary of student online interactions across the entire semester. Participation online was optional, but strongly encouraged and reinforced when the students and instructors met in person.

Table 4: Numbers of Student Online Postings

	Messages Read by student	Messages Posted by student
CLASS MEDIAN	327.00	18.00
CLASS AVERAGE	1102.19	20.95
Class Total	128,969	2,452

Researchers observed a pattern in the risk rubric scores among those students who earned the lowest and highest grades in the class. Students in the lowest 10% (n=12) of the overall course grade consistently showed a low to medium risk score, as compared to the highest scoring 10%, who consistently scored as high risk-takers. A sample of these scores appears in Table 5 below. Low risk-takers may not have been lowest in the number of posts, time online, or messages read; however, how they used the online discussion and the level at which they interacted with their peers and took risks appears to indicate limited engagement in learning during the course of the semester.

Table 5: Online Course Usage of Students with Lowest and Highest Grades

ID	Messages Read	Messages Posted	Total Course Pts *(out of 100)*	Letter Grade	Risk Score	Risk Group
M01	367	17	74.9	C	4	Low
F01	16736	26	89.3	B+	5	L-M
M02	223	4	84.6	B	4	Low
M03	224	3	89.1	B+	5	L-M
F11	430	46	99.5	A	12	M-H
F15	1183	54	100	A	13	High
F17	606	43	99.5	A	12	M-H
F19	384	32	100	A	14	High

Researchers used the modified BLC assessment chart to identify support for BLC features within the students' online postings. The table below (Table 6) offers examples of students' postings that exemplify the BLC concepts based on the indicator examples. It also indicates the percentage of posts that positively support the BCL features. All student quotes are reprinted verbatim. The data in the table below (Table 6) provides clear support for the existence of BLC features. Upon examination of student online postings there are significant trends that positively support the existence of these concepts. For instance, 92% of the sampled student postings displayed the BLC concept of "Shared Goals", 90% supported the concept of "Safe and Supportive Conditions", 92% displayed "Collective Identity", 95% showed "Collaboration", 90% showed "respectful Inclusion" 96% exhibited "Progressive Discourse toward Knowledge Building" and 85% supported "Mutual Appropriation".

Table 6: Student Posting Examples that Support BLC Features

BLC Feature	***Range of Theme Indicators***	***Posts that Support Theme***	***Student Online Posting Examples***
Shared Goals	Students in this class focus on certain goals we have in common. *--to--* Projects and activities give us a nothing to work together that is worthwhile.	92%	*1st student's post:* "I agree...I wish i had some constructive criticism that I could give but I think the summary is great. Really nice job everyone." *2nd student's response:* "I think that summary #2 is well written and ready to post. Kelly did a great job putting together all of our ideas. The summary flows nicely and it expresses clear ideas, as well as solutions to keep track of Scott's behavioral and academic development."
Safe and Supportive Conditions	People feel comfortable expressing their thoughts and ideas. *--to--* I would not take too many risks in this class; not a safe environment.	90%	*1st student's post:* "im a little confused. we identified social interaction as the schools most important concern, however is that considered the the most important academic concern because it is school related? i thought we had to discuss the biggest social and biggest academic concern, i am not sure" *2nd student's response:* "actually, i feel like that improving his social skills and behavior skills is more of a family need, and that a need from the school is making sure that he is receiving proper education and that he is getting the maximized focus of making sure that he is getting a good education. i re-read what we wrote on our team summary, and it seemed more that this is what the needs were with the school and family"

Collective Identity	We enjoy a sense of connection. *--to--* I do not feel like I belong in this class	92%	*1st student's post:* "Did you see Dr. parker's feedback? I told him I thought that we worked really well as a team this semester which allowed us to share and collaborate in a very productive manner. I think we all really learned a lot in completing each team summary and it will definitely prove helpful as we being our student teaching next year. I thanked him for a great semester." *2nd student's response:* "yea thanks for posting it. i have been busy with lacrosse this weekend. it looks great! good job team!" *3rd student's response:* "I think Liz has put it nicely. Thanks again Dr. Parker!" *4th student's response:* "Good work Team & have a great summer!!"
Collaboration	We interact and work together a lot in this class. *--to--* There is not much student-to-student contact in this class.	95%	*1st student's post:* "I was just thinking for another approach to working on his interpersonal skills, maybe he could enroll in a Home-ec class during school? It would be a much smaller setting with fewer people and it would be working on the skills he would need for his future! Any thoughts on that? ..." *2nd student's response:* "I think that's an awesome idea! It is definitely something that he is interested in, and since there's a teacher in the room, he can easily be evaluated." *3rd student's response:* "exactly!!! And then he could get credit for doing assignments and learn about time management Would this be an in school class, or some kind of culinary/catering service thing? Great idea!" *4th student's response:* "Oh wow! I think it would keep him more focused in school if he was spending more time doing things he was interested in! I think something like that would show great progress!" *5th student's response:* "I like the idea...want me to write it up?"

Respectful Inclusion	We respect differences between people. *--to--* Not much effort is made to help everyone fit in.	90%	*1st student's post:"* As a transitional counselor, i think that is obviously important to work on Maria's test-taking skills so that her scores will match her competency in and outside the classroom, however it is also important to focus on the fact that Maria is extremely gifted and unique, and at the same cannot afford college. This is why informing her and her mother about scholarships that are specific for her needs, and talents is extremely important; that way after Maria is given aid regarding help with bettering her scores, and she gets accepted in into a good school, she will also have the means to attend it." *2nd student's response*"yes, I think you are right on track with what we are doing. However, this is not a goal that is observable and measurable, and that we can collect any assessments on. So although it is an important part of Maria's plan and transition in to college, it is not (in my opinion) the two main goals we need to focus on for this assignment."

Progressive Discourse toward Knowledge Building	Our questions and discussions help us build knowledge together. *--to--* I am working on projects to learn for myself.	96%	*1st student's post:* "the draft looks great but dr. parker said something about discussing the importance of these two goals. I don't know what everyone thinks but maybe we should talk about how accomplishing these two goals will eventually help her to get into college and be successful there." *2nd student's response:* "I agree. I believe that increasing her testing skills will help her in college because many of the course assessments, especially earlier in your college career are test-oriented (think about our Gen-Eds and how little creativity in assessment we received to gauge our understanding). Therefore, to increase her testing skills would aid in that way.have enough time to review one-on-one with Maria about her writing. Although they do have services on college campuses, helping Maria get acquainted with assistive tech will surely allow to her be more independent with her writing assignments." *3rd student's response:* "I looked over our summary and edited it some. The changes I made were minor, but might be important, and they are all in bold letters. Lauren posted earlier that Dr. Parker had mentioned we needed to include the importance of the goals, I think Scott did a great job "answering" this in his post. I think we should include this in our summary." *4th student's response:* "That looks really good. I think the way you organized it makes our goals and objectives really clear. I still think that maybe we should add something at the end about these goals eventually helping her out in college. But maybe that is too general of an idea. I'm not really sure what kind of explanation Dr. Parker is looking for. What do you guys think?" *5th student's response:* "I added in a part at the end for why these overall goals are important (in red). Feel free to edit/take them out if you don't see them fit."

Mutual Appropriation	We teach each other a lot in this class, not just relying on the teacher. *--to--* I do what is required for the group.	85%	*1st student's post:* "apologies for not getting it up till now... aaand i have NO idea how to add an attachment as a word document, so if someone knows how please tell me... for now i posted the draft in a separate thingy..." *2nd student's response:* "I believe the way to attach the document is when you post it underneath this box that I am typing in says add attachments and I think that is how you would attach it. Just make sure you have the subject. Is there a separate place you are supposed to post this too or do you just do it under our case study team discussion?" *3rd student's response:* "well, i cut out as much as i could, its still over 3 pages but its less than three and a half so i can live with that. i didnt cut down anything from the roles just cause i thought it was all relevant. thanks for the corrections and suggestions, and ill attach the final summary in a separate post. enjoy the rest of the weekend :)"

The authors examined another data source to assess the sense of community and overall satisfaction students felt about the re-designed course. Standard course evaluation forms were used for this purpose. Overall, the standard course evaluations from 75.2% (n = 88) of the class were very positive. The evaluation form uses a 10-point scale with 10 being outstanding. The table below (Table 7) provides the mean scores:

Table 7: Standard Course Evaluation Comparisons

Evaluation Area	AL and UDI Designed Course (Average)	Department Score (Average)	University Undergraduate Course Score (Average)
Presented material	9.0	8.9	8.6
Organization	9.4	9.0	8.7
Clear Objectives	9.5	9.1	8.7
Fulfilled Objectives	9.2	9.2	8.8
Clear assignments	9.4	9.1	8.7
Graded Fairly	9.2	9.3	8.8
Appropriate Exam	8.9	9.1	8.7
Accessibility	9.4	9.3	8.9
Interest, Concern	9.5	9.3	8.9
Preparation	9.4	9.3	9.0

Student interactions and artifacts from the course support these evaluations and support the decisions made by the design team in constructing and delivering the course content. Analysis of student online interactions and course evaluations clearly indicated evidence that the course design and use of instructional technology allowed the instructional team to achieve our goals.

Educational or Scientific Importance of Study

This study examined online discourse that occurred in a blended course. In redesigning the course, the authors incorporated AL and UDI principles with the belief that the infusion of these design principles would facilitate the emergence of BLCs. Comments by students were positive about this course's design. Additionally, during the last two years, student evaluations about this course remained higher than average scores on both Department and University course evaluations. The themes that emerged from an analysis of the online posts offer strong evidence that design decisions based on AL and UDI principles helped create bounded learning communities. An unexpected finding was the pattern seen in students who scored lowest in the class and their lack of observable risk-taking behavior within the online discourse.

Academic risk-taking specifically involves students' assessment of the known and unknown outcomes of a learning activity as they make choices about their involvement based on possible benefits and consequences. The risks individuals take in making educational decisions may involve actual or perceived risk to self-esteem, success, and well-being (Ely, 1986). This is important in educational environments, since empirical evidence suggests that academic risk-taking among adult learners can support their acquisition of knowledge and skills and result in improved learning motivation and achievement (Clifford, 1991). In addition, academic risk-taking can influence the growth of creativity (Jonassen & Grabowski, 1993), the development of expertise (Daley, 1999), and the cultivation of reflective practice (Ussher, 2001). University instructors may share an interest in pedagogical practices that influence such meaningful learning outcomes, regardless of their academic discipline.

Overall data analysis resulted in numerous indicators of how the new course design supported academic risk-taking amongst many students in the blended environment of EPSY 207. Quantitative and qualitative evidence of risk-taking, formation of community, growth in creativity, and development of special education expertise supports the efficacy of utilizing Adult Learning theories and the Principles of Universal Design for Instruction (UDI) to design and deliver online education. Results from this study also suggest that, to engage *all* students, further research is needed to explore additional methods for encouraging student risk taking in online environments such as "blended" courses.

The authors wish to gratefully acknowledge Dr. Thomas DeFranco and Dr. Marijke Kehrhahn (University of Connecticut) for their visionary administrative support and Dr. Orv Karan (University of Connecticut), who generously provided permission to adapt his case studies for use in EPSY 207.

References

Bonk, C. J., & Graham, C. R. (2005). *Handbook of blended learning: global perspectives, local designs.* . San Francisco, CA: Pfeiffer Publishing.

Bonk, C. J., Hixon, E., & Yamagata-Lynch, L. (2002). The pedagogical TICKIT: web conferencing to promote communication and support during teacher professional development. *Journal of Technology and Teacher Education 10*(2), 205-233.

Brown, J.S. & Duguid, P. (1991). Organizational learning and communities-of-practice: Toward a unified view of working, learning, and innovation. *Organization Science,* 2(1):40-57. Carr, S. (2000). As distance education comes of age, the challenge is keeping the students. [Electronic Version]. *The Chronicle of Higher Education*, 23, A39. Retrieved viewed 11/01/2006 from http://chronicle.com/free/v46/i23/23a00101.htm

Carr, S. (2000). As distance education comes of age, the challenge is keeping the students. *The Chronicle of Higher Education*, 46(23), A39-A41.

Clifford (1991) mentioned on p.35 in book, quote page no. missing

Diaz, D. P. (2002). Online drop rates revisited [Electronic Version]. *The Technology Source [Online]*, May/June. Retrieved 11/06/2006 from http://technologysource.org/article/online_drop_rates_revisited/

Garrison, D.R. and Kanuka, H. (2004). Blended learning: uncovering its transformative potential in higher education. *Internet and Higher Education*, 7(2):95-105.

Greene, J.C., Caracelli, V. J., & Graham, W. F. (1989). Toward a conceptual framework for mixed-method evaluation designs. *Educational Evaluation and Policy Analysis* 11(3), 255-274.

Gutierrez, R. J. (1982). *A Study of the Relation between Locus of Control and Risk Taking for Graduate Students in Education.* Unpublished Masters, California State University, Northridge.

Harasim, L., Hiltz, S. R., Teles, L., & Turoff, M. (1995). *Learning networks: A field guide to teaching and learning online* Cambridge, MA: MIT Press.

Haythornthwaite, C., Kazmer, M., Robins, J., & Shoemaker, S. (2000). Community development among distance learners: Temporal and technological dimensions [Electronic Version]. *Journal of Computer Mediated Communication* 6. Retrieved November 15, 2006 from http://jcmc.indiana.edu/vol6/issue1/haythornthwaite.html.

Herring, S. (1999). Interactional coherence in CMC [Electronic Version]. *Journal of Computer-Mediated Communication*, 4. Retrieved November 18, 2006 from http://jcmc.indiana.edu/vol4/issue4/herring.html.

Holmes, A., Polhemus, L., & Jennings, S. (2005). CATIE: a blended approach to situated professional development. *Journal of Educational Computing Research, 32*(4), 381-394.

Kreijnsa, K., Kirschnerb, P. A., & Jochemsb, W. (2003). Identifying the pitfalls for social interaction in computer-supported collaborative learning environments: a review of the research. *Computers in Human Behavior, 19*, 335-353.

Lapadat, J. C. (2002). Written Interaction: A Key Component in Online Learning. *Journal of Computer-Mediated Communication* 7(4), online.

Lave, J. & Wenger, E. (1991). *Situated learning: legitimate peripheral participation).* Cambridge, UK: Cambridge University Press.

Lundeberg, M. A., & Moch, S. D. (1995). Influence of social interaction on cognition: connected learning in science. *Journal of Higher Education, 66*(3), 310-335.

Merriam, S. B., & Clark, M. C. (1991). *Lifelines: Patterns of work, love, and adulthood.* San Francisco: Jossey-Bass Publishers.

Ponticell, J. A. (2003). Enhancers and inhibitors of teacher risk taking: a case study. *Peabody Journal of Education, 78*(3), 5-24.

Rehn, G. (1990). Flexibility and free choice in working life. In J. Habib & C. Nusberg (Eds.), *Rethinking worklife options for older persons* (pp. 199-215). Washington, D.C. : International Federation on Aging.

Rovai, A. P. (2001). Building classroom community at a distance: a case study [Electronic Version]. *Education Technology Research and Development* 49. Retrieved November 5, 2006 from https://www.aect.org/Intranet/Publications/etrd/4904.html.

Scott, S. S., McGuire, J. M., & Shaw, S. F. (2003). *Principles of Universal Design for Instruction* Storrs: University of Connecticut, Center on Postsecondary Education and Disability.

Snow, R. & Farr, M. (1987). Cognitive-conative-affective processes in aptitude, learning, and instruction: An introduction In R. Snow & M. Farr (Eds.), *Conative and Affective Process Analysis*. Hillsdale, NJ: Erlbaum Associates.

Spitzer, D. R. (1975). Effect of group discussion on teacher attitudes toward risk taking in educational situations. *Journal of Educational Research, 68*, 371-374.

Weber, E. U., Blais, A.-R. E., & Betz, N. E. (2002). Measuring risk perceptions and risk behaviors. *Journal of Behavioral Decision Making, 12*, 263-290.

Whittle, J., Morgan, M., & Maltby, J. (2000). *Higher learning online: Using constructivist principles to design effective asynchronous discussion* Paper presented at the NAWEB 2000 virtual conference from http://naweb.unb.ca/2k/papers/whittle.htm

Wilson, B. G., Ludwig-Hardman, S., Thornam, C. L., & Dunlap, J. C. (2004). *Bounded Community: Designing and Facilitating Learning Communities in Formal Courses*. Paper presented at the American Educational Research Association.

Interactive Learning Technology Improves Engineering Student Competencies

Peter Mark Jansson

Over the past four years (Autumn 2003-Autumn 2006) the development and improvement of a set of interactive learning technologies has been incorporated into the teaching of a set of core electrical and computer engineering (ECE) courses (Networks I and II – covering the fundamentals of DC circuits and AC circuits respectively) at Rowan University in Glassboro, NJ, USA. The results have shown a steady increase in the performance of circuit analysis by the second year ECE students and a significant increase in the quantity of core knowledge imparted during the quarter long sequences during which each course is delivered. This paper describes the interactive technologies - how they are implemented in the didactic environment in the college - and the improvements in student competencies as a result. It is believed the use of these or similar interactive learning technologies may be critical to the active engagement in their own learning of the current generation of students raised in the digital age.

Background for Research

While this author is not primarily engaged in the development and documentation of the scholarship of learning technology, he keeps abreast of the rationale, benefits, innovations and outcomes of that scholarly work. Since this professor teaches engineering students at a university that is primarily a teaching college he continues to try to innovate and improve the delivery of the ECE curriculum through the application of those research findings which attest to increasing student retention of foundational concepts and knowledge in science. This is of prime import to an ECE curriculum which is increasingly pressed to maintain regency with ever evolving and expanding ECE fields while assuring that student competencies with the fundamental concepts, theory, mathematics and core science governing ECE are not diminished. At Rowan University's College of Engineering, a primary means used to meet this challenge is the Engineering Clinic which is described in numerous other papers.[1,2,3,4,5] The Engineering Clinic innovation enables us to cover more material each year to keep pace with the expanding ECE curriculum (and is covered in greater depth in the other cited papers), but the application of active learning technology and techniques described in this research enables us to assure that ECE students are continuing to build a strong and deep foundation in the essential ECE core competencies. The motivation for incorporating these technologies stems from the underlying "paradigm shift that is taking hold in American higher education," from "a college is an institution that exists to provide instruction" to "a college is an institution that exists to produce learning."[6] This fundamental transition in science and engineering education is due, in part, to the significant shift in learning styles and modes for accepting information of the current generation of students entering higher education that have been raised in the digital age. Shorter duration attention spans, exposure to repeated digital stimulation and extended engagement with new technologies (cell phones, text messaging, music videos, television, high frequency visual advertisements, etc.) are considered potential contributors to the decrease in the percentage of modern students in higher education able to effectively absorb sensory information through written or spoken words alone. According to recent research the modality through which sensory information is most effectively perceived is visual (this includes pictures, diagrams, graphs, demonstrations, and field trips)[7-8]. Only about 20% of students find the verbal approaches their most effective modalities for acquiring input data (verbal includes: sounds, written and spoken words, formulas)[7,8,9]., while it has been found that 90-95% of most college course content is verbal.[9] Research indicates that Given our department's goal here in the University and its ABET approved curriculum to "create effective ECE engineers"[1,10], we must maximize their ability perceive the core ECE information, assure it is well rehearsed in their working memory in our courseware and provide the greatest opportunities for it to become encoded within their long-term memory during their 4–year ECE program. This model[11] is based on the research into human cognition by Atkinson and Shiffrin highlighted in Figure 1 below:

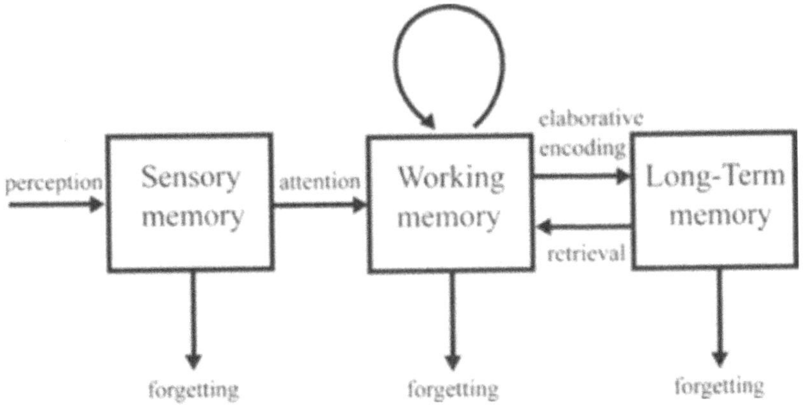

Figure 1: Basic Information-Processing Model of Human Cognition[11]

According to this view, as educators our goal of getting students to comprehend, apply and retain the core ECE knowledge we hope to impart during their educational experience is confounded by a very 'lossy' process. Forgetting seems to be the key leakage from the system described above and it apparently occurs to a very high degree in the very first portion of the model. If only 20% of the students in higher education have verbal input as their most effective modality for acquiring information, then, many of the verbal queues we provide in our lectures and classroom oratory as well as the reading we assign with its associated important concepts and formulae fall on deaf ears 4 of the 5 times. If we desire to get the core concepts into our students working memory and ultimately long-term memory the written and spoken words and formulae alone appear to unable to cross the first threshold into their cognition. This is where active learning technology begins to provide multiple paths for student perception as we compete for their sensory memory. What current researchers in the scholarship of teaching are telling us as educators is that "What professors do in their classes matters far less than what they ask students to do."[12] By actively engaging students in their own learning process, using multiple modalities, assuming they will retain less than one-quarter of what we say or write alone, we have significantly increased the probability that we will have reached their sensory memory and can then, through rehearsal exercises, reach the working memory to apply that perceived knowledge. The primary focus of this paper is not to present the merits of active learning technologies and to describe the many techniques in detail as there are many excellent works[13,14,15,16] that have already adequately addressed that subject. This paper reports the motivation, application and results from one set of interactive learning technologies that have been consistently expanded over the last four years in two core ECE courses to increase student competency and performance. The section which follows describes how the techniques fared when contrasted with our first year control employing no significant active learning technologies.

Introducing Active Learning Technologies in Rowan's College of Engineering

As a new faculty entering Rowan in 2001, like many this professor was very eager to make a significant difference in the lives and education of our students. In the summer of 2002 he was nominated and received a National Science Foundation supported New Century Scholar Fellowship to attend a Teaching, Learning and Academic Career Workshop at Stanford University. This prestigious event brought junior faculty together from engineering education institutions all over the country in order to teach them the most innovative methods for aiding engineering students in their learning experience. A key innovative teaching methodology prescribed during the workshop was active learning. Numerous techniques for implementing active learning were described by researchers whose expertise was educational research in engineering. Two Rowan University Electrical and Computer Engineering who attended the workshop returned energized and enthusiastic about implementing these techniques in our engineering courses. Over the course of the last five years (Autumn semesters 2002, 2003, 2004, 2005 and 2006) the author has kept records of how well each sophomore ECE class of Networks I and II students performed. First with standard active learning exercises and then using the active learning methods that were uniquely developed here at Rowan (called learning checks and learning moments) tailored to ECE sophomores attending Networks I and Networks II courses. These active learning methods verify that engineering students definitely understand more and retain more when engaged in active learning during the semester. The results which follow will further describe the rationale for arriving at this conclusion from the data.

While active learning experiences and techniques are not necessarily new (as described in the previous section), their key integration into engineering pedagogy and utilization every few minutes of lecture so consistently across the entire semester is a key innovation. Students rapidly learn in the course (from the very first lecture beginning for in Autumn 2003 – Networks I) that if they are not paying close attention (moment-by-moment) to what is shown and stated during the lecture they will be unable to correctly answer the learning check which appears on the screen every 6-10 minutes. A key part of this innovative approach is that these learning checks are collected and graded each day/week so the student knows how well they are performing and that these 'checks' are an integral and significant part of their course credit (it is factored into the classroom participation grade). Alternately, if they are paying attention and absorbing the understanding being imparted during the more formal part of the lecture, answering the learning check is often as simple as finishing a sentence or completing a calculation that has already been started by the professor. In this way the learning check is assuring that maximum attention is maintained throughout the 75 minute lecture period. As was clearly illustrated in an experimental study of information retention during a 50-minute lecture, listeners retained 50-70% of the material presented throughout when active learning techniques were employed as compared with a rate that fell from 70% at the beginning of the lecture to 20% by the lecture's end when the more familiar standard oratory style was employed.[17] Today it is more widely known that stand up and deliver lecturing is not as effective on this generation of learners as it was believed to be in the past. The use of active learning methods, while recognized as innovative teaching methodology, are rarely implemented as vigorously as has been done in the past four years in Networks I. Each day students came prepared to pay attention, knowing that at any moment they would be asked to answer a learning check, they found quickly from experience that paying attention and actively thinking about what was being presented was the easiest way to perform excellently on the exercises. This tool was powerful because it not only gave the professor instant feedback on what concepts were clear and which needed further clarification, but because it assure that the professor maintained the undivided attention of a greater percentage of the learners during the class session (clearly a great challenge today for all teachers). Also, this tool gives the students instant feedback that they are "getting it". The learning checks encourage cooperative learning as well. Students feel free in the class to discuss the problem with a peer if they need to and that peer to peer learning is also a key side benefit of the technique. The use of this active learning technique is to engage the students in minds-on, hands-on problem solving while still in the classroom so they can identify questions or gaps in their knowledge before they leave to go home to try to work on their homework problem set. Importantly, the students are also taking a more active role in their own learning process. If they are not understanding the learning checks they have instant feedback that they need to take action before the class gets too far away from this gap or lack of understanding. Having used these learning checks/moments in many lecture settings student information retention greatly increases even in a single topic lectures.

Exactly What is a 'Learning Check'?

Typically, the course instructor uses whiteboard based problems, Microsoft-powerpoint slides and oral lecture materials to conduct the 75 minute Networks I and II classes. Depending on the course content material being covered in a given lesson the learning check can take the form of a question appearing on the MS-powerpoint slide asking for a definition that was previously presented and described. In that case learning the language of an electrical and computer engineer is being reinforced as important. The learning moment may ask students to complete the steps of a process needed to solve a problem. The instructor may be right in the middle of the second example illustrating the previously outlined process when the next question that flashes on slide show asks the students to complete the next step writing it down on their learning check sheet that is collected each week and graded. The learning checks are used for many purposes – primarily to keep students aware and attentive (maximizing the chance they will perceive what is going on in the classroom) and engaged in their own learning process. Hence, the awareness of concepts, knowledge and process moves into their active, working memory in the classroom and through repetition is retained until they can go home and practice the assigned homework problems which are critical to establishing the knowledge in their longer term memory. Learning checks can be a homework problem that instructor has illustrated on the whiteboard which he takes to step 3 out of 5, then stopping to ask the students to complete steps 4 and 5 either collaboratively (with their peers) or alone. These in-class exercises force the students to take an active role in the lectures, they are unable to be passive listeners for more than 10 minutes at a time.

Assessing Student Mastery of Concepts as an Overall Class

The use of the learning checks as an integral part of the Networks I pedagogy within the Electrical and Computer Engineering department has had a significantly positive effect on electrical and computer engineering student performance in the course. In 2002 active learning methods were first introduced to this author, and while recognized as important, only a few elements of these innovative teaching tools were used (the instant feedback of students writing what they did and did not learn as part of the course, and stopping to have students work together collaboratively to solve an in class problem together). Beginning in 2003 the learning check and the methodology associated with it were introduced and rigorously followed through each lecture session of the course. The results over the past four years, summarized below in this research are truly impressive. The table below summarizes the significant improvement in student class performance and retention within ECE over the four years with learning checks as an integral part of the pedagogy (2003, 2004, 2005, 2006) as compared to the year before learning checks (2002) were introduced. From this table it is clear that an average retention improvement of 23% is a positive step as well for a teaching focused engineering institution.

Table 1: Summary of the Student Learning Benefits of Networks I Learning Checks

Year # of Homework	Lab Test Overall	Learning Checks	Failing Overall	Students Grades	Grades	Grades	Grades	# /Course	Grades In Eval	students Retention
Without LCs										
2002	43*	72	81	67	71	N/A	N/A	N/A	10	76.7%
With LCs										
2003	27	80	81	76	78	40	N/G	No	1	96.3%
2004	35	79	91	75	79	73	82	Yes	3	91.4%
2005	29	80	87	77	81	59	83	Yes	3	89.7%
2006	21	78	85	80	84	73	85	Yes	0	100%
Average With LCs	79	86	77	81					94.4%	
Improvement		+9.7%	+6.2%	+14.9%	+14.1%					+23%
N/A – Not Applicable the 2002 classes did not have formal active learning technology										
N/G – Though Learning Checks were incorporated they were not graded and made part of final student evaluation										
* - NOTE: Though this was a larger class size, the students were broken into two cadres for labs										

Assessing Student Perceptions of Learning Checks as an Aid to ECE Concept Mastery

Clearly the impacts on student retention and performance are quite positive, but how well are the students responding to having to spend part of the lecture time in class solving learning checks? Beginning in 2004, the reaction of students was measured via the Course Evaluation. A simple confidential questionnaire administered to all students taking a course to give the instructor and the department feedback on ways the course can be improved. One question asking "how helpful were the learning checks?" was evaluated by the instructor. Of the 31 students responding to the query, 52% rated the learning checks helpful to very helpful, 39% rated them satisfactory, 6% rated them marginally helpful and only 3% (1 student) rated them as not at all helpful. While not overwhelmingly supportive fully 91% of the students found them to be a satisfactory to very helpful part of their learning resources in 2004. Students rated learning checks as of higher value to their understanding of course materials than the text book and the laboratories for this course. There clearly is not any strong negative rejection to the method. Some student comments supporting the benefits they perceived in learning checks follow, but of key import: of the 31 students completing the survey 27 actually took the time to write some feedback comment (active learning clearly has increased the feedback as well). A very high (and comparable) degree of feedback was provided in 2005 and 2006 as well. Here are some sample relevant comments regarding learning checks from Networks I students (by year):

2004: “The labs and learning checks are helpful and should be continued.”
2004: “Learning checks make you pay attention.”
2005: “The learning checks kept me focused.”
2005: “I believe the learning checks were extremely useful.”
2005: “The most helpful things were the learning checks and homework”
2006: “The learning checks made me pay attention and follow the lectures.”
2006: “The learning checks immediately apply the information.”

Table 2, on the page which follows, shows the overall student survey response to the specific course evaluation question of the how helpful the students perceived the learning checks were as an aid to their understanding the subject matter. It is significant that in nearly all years over 90% of students felt they provided at least some value – and nearly 85% found them a satisfactory to very helpful aid.

During 2004 in response to an open-ended question: “What things about this class should be continued?” 11 Networks I students actually took the time to write in “everything (n=3)” or specifically “the learning checks (n=8)”. In 2005 and 2006, 6 students and 5 respectively noted learning checks in response to an open ended question: “What elements of the course were most helpful in your mastery of DC circuits and systems?”

Table 2: ECE Networks I Student Responses on the Helpfulness of Learning Checks

	2004	2005	2006	Overall	
not at all	1	3	1	5	6.8%
Marginally	2	1	3	6	8.1%
Satisfactorily	13	5	5	23	31.1%
Helpful	9	8	8	25	33.8%
very helpful	6	5	4	15	20.3%
N =	31	22	21	74	
% positive	97%	86%	95%	93%	

While Networks II was never taught without active learning technology it is not as easily estimated how well student performance increased on tests, assignments, labs and homework because of their aid. The comments below indicate they found them helpful.

2004: “Keep the learning checks.”
2004: “The learning checks were helpful.”
2005: “The learning checks were very helpful”
2005: “Continue the learning checks because they make you think instead of just copying notes. Plus it helps you understand the concepts better”
2005: “Learning checks keep you in class discussion.”
2006: “Keep everything.”

Of all the written comments in the course evaluations received regarding learning checks in the three years of surveying in Networks II, 23 students (79.3%) wrote supportive comments and 6 (20.7%) wrote requesting learning checks not be included in the course in the future. It is important to note that in open ended sections of the survey generally only the most outspoken critics, or advocates, take the time to write. All the students who specifically told the professor they did not support learning checks, were not working at passing the course successfully.

Finally the chart illustrated by Table 3 below, confirms that Networks II students also provide resounding support for the benefits of the technology in their learning. In all three years of their use 90% or more of the students (93.7% on average) found the active learning technology at least marginally helpful in their mastery of ECE concepts and problem solving

Table 3: ECE Networks II Student Responses on the Helpfulness of Learning Checks

	2004	2005	2006	Overall	
not at all	1	1	2	4	6.3%
Marginally	5	1	1	7	10.9%
Satisfactorily	6	8	7	21	32.8%
Helpful	9	7	8	24	37.5%
very helpful	3	3	2	8	12.5%
N =	24	20	20	64	
% positive	96%	95%	90%	94%	

Covering More Ground in the Same Quarter

One of the greatest challenges of foundation courses in any subject is to provide a broad and deep enough footing for the students to launch from into their more detailed courses which depend upon a strong and rigorous understanding of the fundamentals. Active learning technology enables students to master more concepts more quickly because of how they work to maintain a high degree of attention while exercising the student's active/working memory and forcing its interplay with longer term memory functions. As a result the number of chapter sections and the associated materials covered has been increased over the years since active learning techniques were developed and are continually refined. Table 4 below indicates how many topic areas were covered in each year in Networks I and II plus the assigned problems completed. It is important to point out that while grades rose or remained constant for these course offerings, this higher quantity of material covered is an indicator of success, since greater material breadth and depth were tested and assigned in these subsequent years.

Table 4: ECE Topics Covered in Networks I and II (2002-2006)[18]

Year	Networks I		Networks II	
	Chapter Sections Completed	HW Problems Completed	Chapter Sects Completed	HW Problems Completed
2002 *	28	99	---	---
2003	33	126	---	---
2004	32	131	25	85
2005	33	127	26	84
2006	42	152	29	99
Improvement Last over First	+14 (50%)	+53 (54%)	+4 (16%)	+14 (16%)
* - No active learning technologies were employed in 2002				

As illustrated above compared with the Networks I course offering (2002) which employed no active learning the quantity of course material covered in the quarter was less. Even with the lower volume of chapter sections (and associated homework) and resulting less material in the tests the grades of the students were poorer overall (see Table 1). By 2006, as the techniques were refined the volume of material covered rose 50% in Networks I and 16% in Networks II. In Networks I overall student grades with the increased content also rose from 71 (C-) (in 2002) to 84 (B) (in 2006). This is an astounding 18% improvement on more challenging tests, labs and assignments. It is clear that higher expectations often create higher performance, but this data confirms that the competencies have expanded and performance increased with the use of active learning technologies.

Correlating Individual Student Performance on Learning Checks with Final Performance

As a class, and overall, the use of these active learning experiences have shown improvements in performance on tests, homework and all measurable indices of student ECE competency. In addition, the confidential classroom participation survey data indicates that students are quite positively aware of the personal benefit they achieve by completing the learning exercises. The previous section even notes that a greater amount of material has been able to be digested and understood over time in long (75 minute) lecture periods, but how well does a student's performance on the active learning technology exercises predict the student's performance individually in the class overall. This section shows that there is a correlation, though not a strong one, between students' scores on their active learning exercises and the final grade they receive in the course (the final evaluation of their competency in the ECE material presented). As is clear from the regression lines for Figures 2 and 3 there is a positive slope to the 'best fit' line. Unfortunately, the equation of the regression is only able to account for 46% of the variance in the data (Networks I only, n=84) and 38% of the entire set of data points (Networks I and II, n =156). This is understandable as some students choose to not turn in their learning exercises for grading (it only represents a few percentage points of total grade) and receive a lower score on that portion while they are still able to pass the course. And we also have students who diligently work on successfully completing their learning checks and still are unable to perform excellently in closed book testing. Nonetheless, if we place a +/- 10 point boundary above and below the regression lines we find that this broader swath includes over 82% of all the data points. There is a modest correlation between a student's active learning score and their final course grade.

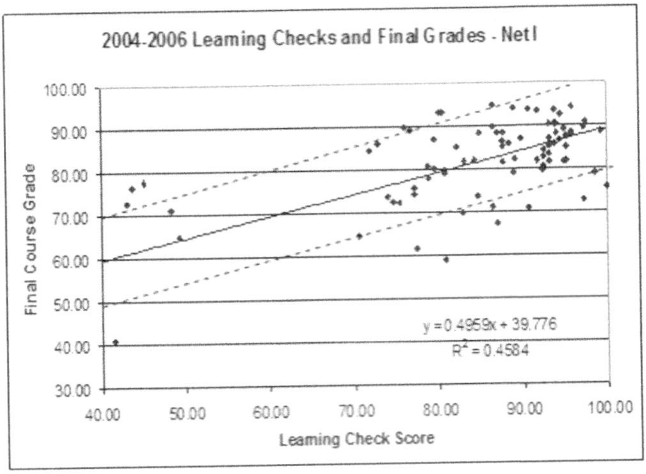

Figure 2 : Correlation Between Learning Exercise Success and Final Grade Networks I (2004-2006), n=84

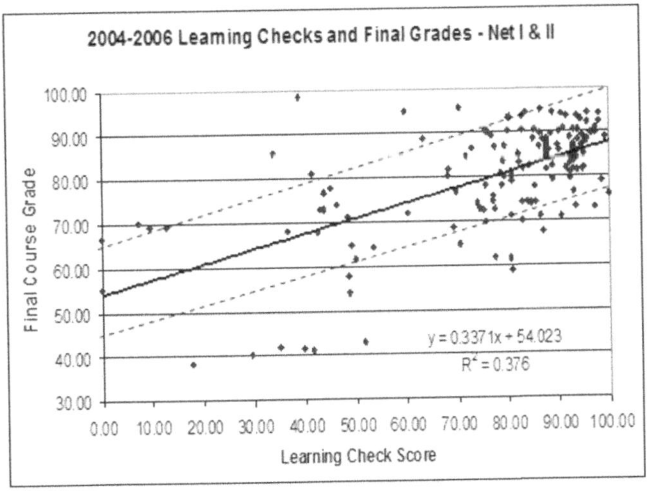

Figure 3 : Correlation Between Learning Exercise Success and Final Grade Networks I and II (2004-2006), n=156

What Have We Learned?

It does appear that Halpern and Hakel are right: "What ***professors do*** in their classes matters far less than what they a***sk students to do.***"[12] The more we forced our ECE sophomore students to be 'active' in the lecture experience the more they could accomplish in homework, lab and on examinations. They covered more materials and they performed better while accomplishing it. Their confidence has increased and they are better prepared to face their remaining ECE curriculum. They also felt more confident interacting with the professor and lab assistant in asking queries and providing candid and honest feedback. The ECE program at Rowan University (founded in 1997) just received its second ABET accreditation in 2006, and as part of our preparations, we contacted our alumni to inquire as to whether they and their employers believed we had created effective ECE engineers through our curriculum. We were amazed by the response. First, over 50% of the alumni responded to our email survey, in addition they volunteered to have us contact their employers or graduate advisors for feedback as well. We found that fully 100% were gainfully occupied (in professional work or grad school). In addition, over 50% of them had gone on for a Master's degree or a PhD exceeding our expectations on our goal of creating lifelong learners. Our alumni graded us via the survey as exemplary in all our core ABET criteria, and believed their education had served them extremely well compared to their peers in creating an effective engineer. We received 100% corroboration of that from their employers as well who said they were performing as a capable engineer in all the areas we have established in our ECE program. The results of the survey have been summarized in the ECE Self Study for ABET cited earlier.[10] It appears that active learning unlocks a motivation in students to inquire, the true essence of all education. We are grateful to participate and observe as the next generation turns on their lights.

Acknowledgements

The author wishes to thank you for the opportunity to present this important teaching innovation developed here at Rowan University to you for your consideration. In addition, thanks must be given to Rowan University, the College of Engineering and the Department of Electrical and Computer Engineering its current chair, Dr. Shreekanth Mandayam and former and founding chair Dr John Schmalzel, PE. without whom support and resources for this work would not have been possible. Finally the ECE sophomore classes of 2002, 2003, 2004, 2005 and 2006, the 150+ students who participated in this research as we all attempted to maximize the benefits they received from participating in Networks I and II during the past 5 years, without them this work would not have been a success.

References

1. Jansson, P.M., Tang, G., Ramachandran, R., Schmalzel, J.; Mandayam, S., Krchnavek, R., Head, L.; Polikar, R. and Ordonez, R., The Role of the Engineering Clinic in Promoting an Agile ECE Learning Environment, ASEE 2006 Annual Conference, Chicago, June 2006
2. J. L Schmalzel, A. J. Marchese, J. Mariappan and S. A. Mandayam, The Engineering Clinic: A four-year design sequence, presented at the 2nd An. Conf. of Nat. Collegiate Inventors and Innovators Alliance, Washington, D.C., 1998.
3. J. L Schmalzel, A. J. Marchese and R. P. Hesketh, What's brewing in the Clinic?, *HP Engineering Educator*, 2:1, Winter 1998, pp. 6-7.
4. C.S. Slater, T.R. Chandrupatla, R.A. Dusseau, and J.L. Schmalzel, Development of multifunctional laboratories in a new engineering school, *Proc. ASEE An. Conf. and Exhibition*, Washington, D.C., 23-26 June 1996.
5. J.L. Schmalzel, T.R. Chandrupatla, R.A. Dusseau, Z. Otero-Keil, and J.H. Tracey, Redesigning the engineering curricula: Combining the best features, *Proc. ASEE Gulf-Southwest Reg. Conf.*, San Antonio, TX, 27-29 Mar 1996, pp. 615-8.
6. Barr, R.D. and Tagg, J., From teaching to learning – A new paradigm for undergraduate education, (1995) Change, Nov./Dec., p. 13-25.
7. Teaching Science: What the Research Tells Us, On the Cutting Edge – Professional Development for Geoscience Faculty, Science Education Research Center @ Carleton College, Online Available: http://serc.carleton.edu/NAGTWorkshops/careerprep/teaching/learning.html
8. Dunbar, R.W., Presentation to 2005 Preparing for an Academic Career Workshop, Pennsylvania State University, 21-24 July, 2005.
9. Felder, R.M. Reaching the Second Tier - Teaching and Learning Styles in College Science Education (1993) Journal of College Science Teaching, v. 23, p. 286-290.
10. Rowan University-Department of Electrical and Computer Engineering 2006 ABET Self-Study, May 2006, Glassboro, NJ:
11. Ambrose, S., What do we know about how students learn? Presentation to New Century Scholars Engineering Faculty Workshop, Stanford University, July, 2002.
12. Halpern, D.F. and Hakel, M.D., Applying the Science of Learning to the University and Beyond (2003) Change, July/Aug., pp.36-41.
13. Felder, R.M. and Brent, R., Navigating the bumpy road to student-centered instruction. (1996) College Teaching, 44(2), p. 43-47.
14. National Research Council, Science Teaching Reconsidered: A Handbook (1997), National Academy Press, Washington, D.C. 88p.

15. Johnson, D.W., Johnson, R.T. and Smith, K.A., (1998) Active learning: Cooperation in the college classroom (2nd ed.) Edina, MN, Interaction Book Co.
16. King, A., From sage on the stage to guide on the side. (1993), College Teaching, 41(1), pp. 30-35
17. McKeachie, W., (1994) Teaching tips, 9th ed., Lexington, MA, Heath & Company
18. Jansson, P.M., Networks I and II Course Websites: Online Available: http://users.rowan.edu/~jansson

Virtual Face-to-Face Communication and the Learning Experience of Post-Graduate Students Studying via Flexible Delivery Mode

Kate Thomson, Boon-Kiang Tan and Christopher Brook

The Centre for International Health (CIH) at Curtin University of Technology delivers its postgraduate courses primarily via flexible delivery mode. This study aimed to determine the necessity, practicality and effectiveness of implementing virtual online face-to-face communication between students and their tutor. Two units were used as case exemplars for this study. Both units promoted virtual face-to-face communication through Skype or MSN during the teaching semester, in addition to email support. The tutor recorded her experience throughout the semester, including students' details, duration of contact and difficulties encountered. Students' experiences were assessed using an online survey, with a hyperlink sent to students' preferred email addresses. Demographic data were collated to allow for an investigation of their effect on student perception and uptake of services. The survey explored student perception of current services and communication, their experience of flexible delivery mode, and their uptake of and experience of virtual online face-to-face communication. Results indicated most students were satisied with email communication, but they believe additional support services and opportunities for communication would enhance their learning experience. The experience of those who communicated through Skype was generally positive, and they reported a higher level of engagement. There is support for further implementation, as the service would likely be utilised by a small proportion of students (those who feel isolated or are dissatisfied with email communication), which would create a manageable increase in the tutor's workload. For students located outside Australia, this provides a financially viable alternative to international telephone communication.

There are issues surrounding the economic sustainability of the current methodology used in the provision of traditional higher education, and the flexible mode of delivery has received interest from institutions as a more viable alternative (Bridgland & Blanchard, 2001). Additionally, non-traditional modes of study that grant students control over their learning experience are attractive to the ever-diversifying student body (Elison-Bowers et al, 2008; Leach & Walker, 2000). Although flexible delivery commonly appeals to international students and dispersed population, it is increasingly preferred by students who live close to their university campus, as it provides them the opportunity to learn at a time and place of their choice (Bridgland & Blanchard, 2001). Research has found both similarities and differences between those who did and did not study through the flexible delivery mode; in terms of characteristics, levels of satisfaction and interaction, and learning experience (Elison-Bowers et al, 2008; Richardson & Price, 2003). The literature recommends that universities look to future technologies, and the provision of various learning options, to ensure they do not disadvantage any group of students (Bonk & King, 1998; Leach & Walker, 2000).

Higher Education and Flexible Delivery

Higher Education has traditionally entailed hundreds of students sitting in a lecture hall for several hours each week, spending additional time at on-campus libraries and joining an array of student organisations. Today, this is supplemented with students who may never visit a university campus, but complete their entire program of study through flexible delivery and interact with their educators almost exclusively through Computer Mediated Communication (CMC) (Richardson & Price, 2003). Computer Mediated Communication was originally designed to increase connectivity (Hiltz & Turoff, 1985) and has grown to include synchronous chat and computer conference systems, email, newsgroups, support networks, bulletin boards and homepages (Khan, 2005), and more recently, social network sites such as 'MySpace' and 'Facebook' (Ellison, Steinfeld & Lampe, 2007).

The flexible delivery of Higher Education is a changing paradigm and influenced by educators, students and technology (Muirhead & Betz, 2005). Early examples of flexible delivery were in Europe (1856) and America (1873), where educators and students exchanged learning materials via post (McKenzie, Christensen & Rigby, 1968; Simonson, Smaldino, Albright & Zvacek, 2000). Flexible delivery has evolved to include a variety of modes, from those similar to the late 19th century, to exclusively online learning. Taylor (1995; 2000) summarised some characteristics of flexible delivery that he believed affect the quality of teaching and learning. Flexibility of time, place and pace of learning characterised earlier models. Interactive delivery was then prioritised over flexibility, and it was not until the flexible learning model that flexibility and interactive delivery were brought together (Taylor, 1995; 2000). The model of *flexible delivery* offered in Higher Education today offers students a combination of internet-based access to online resources and CMC. Flexible delivery creates an opportunity for a change in the role of educators; from providers of information to facilitators of the learning experience (Berge, 2007; Nichols & Gardner, 2002).

Key advantages of flexible delivery are student control over the time, pace and place of their learning (Bridgland & Blanchard, 2001). While this is benficial, some of the issues associated with flexible delivery are the lack of organisational support at faculty and/or institutional level; requirements for additional resources and minimal or nonexistent face-to-face communication (Nichols & Gardner, 2002). This study sought to explore the interaction between tutor and students facilitated by CMC and its influence on the teaching and learning experience.

Higher Education Students

Students' needs, their educator's style and institutional support, can impact on their learning experience (Bridgland & Blanchard, 2001; Khan, 2005; Richardson & Price, 2003). Institutions with a large number of students from lower socio-economic backgrounds and a highly diverse student population find it more challenging to enhance the learning experience (Yorke et al, 2005). An increasingly diverse student body may require universities to shift from an 'integration approach' (integrating students into a particular academic culture) toward a more learner-centred 'adaptation approach', where institutions adapt their administrative and academic cultures to meet the various learning patterns, abilities and interests of a heterogeneous student body (Zepke et al, 2005).

Research consistently shows that student characteristics such as gender, age, cultural background and academic ability, can significantly impact performance on measures relating to academic achievement (Yorke et al, 2005). Student characteristics influence the learning needs and uptake of services provided. For example, age has been shown to influence use of Web Course Tools (WebCT) and use of WebCT can affect performance (Hoskins & van Hoof, 2005). Generally, female students have also been shown to have superior learning outcomes to male students (Yorke et al, 2005). Variables such as cultural background, previous educational experience and current circumstances affect the level of support and contact desired by students (Frank, Toland & Schenk, 2004; Simpson, 2000) and educators should provide appropriate support for all students (Hiltz & Johnson, 1990; Smith & Smith, 1999).

The literature recommends research into developing online environments that not only enhance learning outcomes, but also appeal to a diverse student population (Leach & Walker, 2000). Kember (2007) argues for further research; in particular, explorations of combining online courses with face-to-face communication to enhance students' learning experience. There is support for systems that emphasise pedagogy over technology (Bonk & King, 1998; Bridgland & Blanchard, 2001) as technological enhancements do not automatically transfer to improvements in students' learning experience (Kember, 2007). As many students, particularly those studying through flexible delivery mode, may have time, financial and personal constraints limiting their ability to adapt to change; new technologies imposed should contribute to positive outcomes rather than additional challenges (Elison-Bowers et al, 2008). Thus, it is imperative that support strategies be trialled prior to implementation to determine their practicality and feasibility, particularly from the student perspective (Nichols & Gardner, 2002).

The current study

The Centre for International Health (CIH) at Curtin University of Technology has been recognised for demonstrating a consistently outstanding performance in teaching and learning. Student feedback, in addition to other measures, indicated that they exhibit best practice in flexible delivery. According to figures from the 2007 Curtin Annual Student Satisfaction Survey, students studying through flexible delivery mode are satisfied with services overall (CASS, 2008). The current study gave students the opportunity to provide CIH with recommendations for improvements to existing services or additional services, such as CMC tools. For CIH staff to continue to meet the needs of students and exhibit best practice in flexible delivery, it is important they support innovative measures such as CMC.

As CIH caters primarily to those studying through flexible delivery mode, they should be aware of students' perceptions of current support in order to determine future initiatives. The current atmosphere in the Higher Education sector, technological developments, and the advancement of CIH are substantial drivers for research like this. This research sought to determine the necessity, practicality and effectiveness of implementing virtual online face-to-face communication between individual postgraduate students and their tutor. The authors were also interested in students' uptake, perceptions, and experience of this mode of communication; particularly in terms of their learning experience. This study has the potential to inform the application of CMC in Higher Education and enhance the teaching and learning experience of educators and students.

Method

This study was conducted over a 14-week semester from July to November 2008. The sample chosen for participation were students enrolled in two units offered via flexible delivery mode by CIH. These two units were selected as they generally have reasonable enrolment rates. Although this was not a large sample, virtual online face-to-face communication requires investigation before broad implementation, as it may not be practical or desirable for students or educators. Therefore, this sample was considered sufficient for an exemplar case study.

In the first week of semester, the tutor emailed students to promote CMC as an alternative mode of communication. Students were asked to organise a mutually convenient date and time with the tutor before they attempted to 'chat' via Skype or MSN. A one-page summary of the study, outlining its aims, objectives and methodology, was provided to all students enrolled in the two units. This summary stated that the opinions and information provided by participants would be kept strictly confidential and that information used in the final report would be presented in such a way that the source could not be identified. Students were informed they had the right to withdraw from the study at any time. The contact details of the researchers were provided in case students had questions or concerns with the research.

The enrolled students were sent a link to a questionnaire on the SurveyMonkey website in their penultimate week of semester. To minimise the time taken to complete the survey, the majority of questions were categorical. However, many questions also included an optional freeform response to allow students to provide additional information. The content of the online questionnaire is presented as Appendix 1.

The survey explored student perception of current services and communication, their experience of flexible delivery mode; and their uptake of and experience of virtual online face-to-face communication. Demographic data were collated to allow for an investigation of their effect on student perception and uptake of services, such as sex, age, country of residence, previous and current studies. In addition to the student survey, the tutor also kept a record throughout semester of the number of students who requested an appointment, the time spent with each student, and issues encountered. SPSS software was used to analyse the frequencies and a thematic analysis was conducted on the qualitative responses.

This study had the approval of Curtin University of Technology Human Research Ethics Committee (HR CIH 5-2008).

Results

Thirty-one students responded to the questionnaire, of a possible 42, giving a response rate of 74%. The majority of students surveyed were female, living in Australia and identified as having an Australian background (26 of 31 students). Their ages ranged from 20 to 55. Eighty-one percent (N=25) were older than 25 and 48% (N=15) were older than 35 years of age. Eighty-seven percent (N=27) of the respondents worked in paid employment. Table 1 provides a summary of the characteristics of the participants.

Table 1: Summary of Student Characteristics

Percentages represent the proportion of students that responded to the survey, of the total number of students enrolled.

Variable	Number of respondents	Number who used CMC
Gender		
Male	N=5 (12 %)	N= 0
Female	N=26 (62 %)	N= 4
Age Groups		
20-29	N= 12	N= 2
30-39	N= 7	N= 2
40-49	N= 10	N= 0
50+	N= 2	N= 0
Course enrolled		
International health	N= 15 (100 %)	N= 3
Nursing	N= 16 (52 %)	N= 1
Country of Residence		
Australia	N= 27	N= 1
Europe	N= 1	N= 1
Asia	N= 1	N= 1
Pacific region	N= 2	N= 1
Employment		
Part-Time	N= 17	N= 2
Full- Time	N= 10	N= 2

When asked the reasons for not making use of the additional communication offered, seven students reported their lack of a camera and/or microphone, and three indicated their slow internet speed. Four students (13%), three of whom were aged 47 and above, reported they were uncomfortable with the technology. However, 16 students (52%) indicated they had no need for the additional CMC as they were satisfied with the current communication and support services provided by Curtin University and CIH. Three students responded that they did not know that CMC was offered. As only 4 of the 31 (13%) students utilised the CMC, the sample was too small to determine any relationship between students' characteristics such as age or cultural background, and their uptake of the tool offered.

The results of the students' experience with CMC and the potential use of CMC are summarised in Table 2.

Table 2: Summary of Student Experience

	Strongly Agree	Agree	Neither agree nor disagree	Disagree	Strongly Disagree	N/A	No response
I believe this communication affected my learning experience in a positive way	3 (10%)	4 (13%)	9 (29%)	1 (3%)	1 (3%)	10 (32%)	3 (10%)
I believe this communication better prepared me for the assignments	3 (10%)	1 (3%)	9 (29%)	3 (10%)	1 (3%)	11 (35%)	3 (10%)
I believe this communication assisted with the learning outcomes of the unit	2 (6%)	3 (10%)	8 (26%)	3 (10%)	1 (3%)	11 (35%)	3 (10%)
I would like this opportunity for communication made available in other units	4 (13%)	12 (39%)	5 (16%)	1 (3%)	1 (3%)	5 (16%)	3 (10%)
I would use additional modes of communication, such as online face-to-face communication via Skype or MSN, if they were available in other units	3 (10%)	8 (26%)	8 (26%)	4 (13%)	1 (3%)	4 (13%)	3 (10%)

Seven students agreed this communication enhanced their learning experience. Although a high proportion of respondents indicated that the questions related to the learning experience and learning outcomes did not apply to them or they responded *neither agree nor disagree*, there was support for implementation of this communication. Sixteen (52%) of students indicated they would like CMC such as Skype or MSN to be made available in other units and 11 (35%) said they would use such communication if offered.

Students were also given the opportunity to comment on their experience of flexible delivery mode and CMC. The four students who used the communication offered found it to be a positive experience. For example, one student commented:

"The tutor was very responsive to email communication, which meant that I did most of my communicating with her through that. I used Skype to ask specific questions that were a bit complicated and hard to explain over email." [Student living in Asia, aged 30]

Another student commented: *"Great to have verbal contact with tutor and also face to face. I could really understand the information she was giving me".* [Student living in the Pacific region, aged 33]

This study intended to trial CMC and provide insight into students' experience of their course, and many of the students commented favourably. Their positive experience was best exemplified by the comment made by a student living in Europe:

"I feel that during my distance education study with Curtin that I have had more contact with my tutors than I did during my undergraduate degree that I did internally (at a different university). I have found that Curtin has offered good communication methods (email, telephone and Skype) and I am very happy with the way my course is provided." [Post graduate student in International Health]

The tutor estimated her time managing both units to be approximately 50 hours for the semester, not including time spent marking assignments. This comprised a welcome email, and telephone and email communication with students throughout the semester. Her time spent implementing Skype and MSN communication totalled three hours over the semester, indicating that the addition of this CMC did not increase her teaching workload significantly. The tutor also indicated that when addressing complex questions she preferred MSN/Skype (if available to students) or telephone communication, as she found email more time consuming.

Discussion

This study provided an exemplar case study of the practicality and effectiveness of offering virtual online face-to-face communication to post-graduate students studying via flexible delivery mode. Four (13%) of the 42 enrolled students used the CMC offered, and 16 (52%) indicated they would like to see similar communication offered in other units, and for Curtin University and CIH to continue to provide quality support services. The following discussion is not intended to be definitive, as the limitations of the sample size and sampling must be taken into account. However, the results can be considered indicative of the population of post-graduate Health Sciences students

The tutor considers the advantages of offering such communication, and her own and the students' experience of the communication outweigh the minimal additional time required to implement the tool. Some of the barriers to the implementation of this tool in other units could be resolved with increased support around its uptake; some students indicated they would use CMC with assistance. Despite repeated emails and announcements on WebCT, there were students who did not use CMC as they did not know it was available, so wider promotion would be necessary.

Similar studies done on undergraduate students have had a higher level of uptake, so it may be that older post-graduate students are less inclined to adopt new technology. None of the students who accessed CMC were older than 35, so age may have been a confounding variable. The current group of undergraduate students is more inclined to trial, even seek new technologies and alternate methods of communication, and as they move into post-graduate study, they may expect a variety of forms of CMC with their tutor, creating a greater demand for tools such as Skype.

Internet speed and not having a camera or microphone were also reported as reasons for students not utilising the service. Consideration should be given to groups of students who will not be supported by this communication. The benefits of offering CMC are reduced if remote and/or technologically limited locations further disadvantage students, leading to increased feelings of isolation, and a diminished, rather than enhanced learning experience (Bates, 2005).

Although some students gave their lack of equipment as reason for not using CMC, 16 (52%) said they had no need for this form of communication. This may have been due to their having previously completed a tertiary qualification, or because they already felt well supported by the university. As the majority of students who did not access CMC live in Australia, and three of the four students who accessed the service live overseas, our findings support those of Ludwig-Hardman and Dunlap (2003), who found isolation influences the level of support desired by students. The cost of a local call within Australia may be minimal and the convenience of picking up the phone to contact the tutor may explain why there was less uptake of this CMC by students who live in Australia. In contrast, the cost of an international call may be prohibitive and the use of Skype and MSN, which does not incur additional financial cost, may be a more attractive option of communication for students who live overseas.

Face-to-face communication has the advantage of both verbal and non-verbal signals, providing multiple opportunities for clarification of meaning; whereas forms of CMC such as email do not provide the same set of signals (DeVito, 2008). Several students commented that CMC was useful for questions that were not suited to email. Collis and Moonen (2007) argue blended courses are best, with face-to-face contact provided at least once; they assert seeing and hearing educators facilitates students' interpretation of subsequent written feedback. Real time or synchronous CMC is important for interaction between educators and non campus-based students (Shih, Hung, Ma & Jin, 2007). Although only four students used the communication, seven indicated it had positively affected their learning experience, suggesting that the use and availability of a service can improve the students' experience.

The study aimed to assess students' uptake, perceptions and experience of CMC. As only a few students made use of CMC, this could be perceived as an unnecessary service to offer, and confirmation that Curtin University and CIH are meeting the needs of students. However, CMC's practicality and effectiveness as a communication tool are reflected in the positive experience of the tutor and students who used it. It may be that the necessity of such a tool is of less importance than its potential to enhance the learning experience of students. Although this study is unable to provide evidence that this form of CMC will improve student learning, it has demonstrated that students have positive learning experiences when well supported and provided with adequate opportunities for communication with their tutor.

Although many students did not require CMC, some students may have been more inclined to use it had they owned the necessary equipment. Further implementation might involve requiring students to purchase a headset, as is the case for students studying a Graduate Diploma of Midwifery, which has a blended teaching approach (Morrow, Phillips & Bethune, 2007). A couple of the students gave their reason for not using CMC as their uneasiness with the technology, so a manual that explains step-by-step how to use Skype, MSN or similar software should be provided to students to facilitate their use.

Future studies could target the students' response to different tutors. Some tutors may be less equipped to ensure student experience of CMC is positive. Academic staff are often encouraged, rather than supported, to implement CMC (Barber & Wilkinson, 2005). This study focused on the student experience of CMC, but further research could explore the impact of staff development on both tutors' and students' experience of CMC.

Conclusion

This case exemplar indicates that CMC can be practically and effectively implemented to improve the level of engagement between a tutor and postgraduate students. In this study, few students chose to utilise the CMC but those who did, had a positive experience. Students indicated they would use this service if they needed to and they considered it potentially useful to enhance their learning experience.

References

Barber, W. & Wilkinson, M. (2005). The change in academic skill base required for the transition from face-to-face teaching to blended delivery. Paper presented at ODLAA Breaking down Boundaries, 17th Biennial Conference of the Open and Distance Learning Association of Australia, 9-11 November 2005, Adelaide, South Australia. Paper available from http://www.odlaa.org/events/2005-conf/nonref/odlaa2005BarberWilkinsonAbstract.pdf

Bates, A.W. (2005). Technology, E-learning and Distance Education. London: Routledge.

Berge, Z.L. (2007). Motivate and Manage: Key Activities of Online Instructors. In J.M. Spector (Ed.), *Finding your Online Voice: Stories Told by Experienced Online Educators* (pp.73-82). New Jersey: Lawrence Erlbaum Associates.

Bonk, C.J. & King, K.S. (1998). *Electronic Collaborators: Learner Centered technologies for Literacy, Apprenticeship and Discourse*. Mahwah, New Jersey: Lawrence Erlbaum Associates.

Bridgland, A.C. & Blanchard, P. (2001). Flexible delivery/ flexible learning: ... does it make a difference?. *Australian Academic and Research Libraries, 32*(3), 177-191.

CASS (2008). Curtin Annual Student Satisfaction Survey (CASS) - Report 2007. Published February 2008. Retrieved June 19, 2008, from http://planning.curtin.edu.au/local/docs/CASS_report_2007.pdf

Collis, B. & Moonen, J. (2007). The Contributing Student: Philosophy, Technology and Strategy. In J.M. Spector (Ed.), *Finding your Online Voice: Stories Told by Experienced Online Educators* (pp.19-32). New Jersey: Lawrence Erlbaum Associates.

DeVito, J. A. (2008). *Human Communication: The Basic Course* (11th ed.). New York: Allyn & Bacon.

Elison-Bowers P., Snelson C., Casa de Calvo, M. & Thompson, H. (2008). Health science students and their learning environment: a comparison of perceptions of on-site, remote-site, and traditional classroom students [online]. *Perspectives in health information management / AHIMA, American Health Information Management Association, 5*(2).

Ellison, N.B., Steinfield, C. & Lampe, C. (2007). The benefits of Facebook "friends": Social capital and college students' use of online social network sites [online]. *Journal of Computer-Mediated Communication, 12*(4), article 1. Retrieved July 3, 2008, from http://jcmc.indiana.edu/vol12/issue4/ellison.html

Frank, J., Toland, J. & Schenk, K. (2004). The Effect of Culture on Email Use: Implications for Distance Learning. In C. Howard, K. Schenk & R. Discenza (Eds.), *Distance Learning and University Effectiveness: Changing Educational Paradigms for Online Learning.* Chapter XI (pp. 213-233). London: Information Science Publishing.

Hiltz, S. & Johnson, K. (1990). User Satisfaction with Computer-Mediated Communication Systems. *Management Science, 36*(6), 739-764.

Hiltz, S. & Turoff, M. (1985). Structuring Computer-Mediated Communication Systems to avoid information overload. *Communications of the Association for Computing Machinery 28*(7), 680-689.

Hoskins, S.L., & van Hoof, J.C. (2005). Motivation and ability: which students use online learning and what influence does it have on their achievement? *British Journal of Educational Technology, 36*(2), 177-192.

Kember, D. (2007). *Reconsidering open and distance learning in the Developing World-Meeting students' learning needs.* New York: Routledge.

Khan, B. (2005). *Managing E-Learning: Design, Delivery, Implementation and Evaluation.* London: Information Sciences Publishing.

Leach, K. & Walker, S. (2000). Internet Based Distance Education: Barriers, Models, and New Research. In *Proceedings of WebNet World Conference on the WW and Internet* (pp.903-905). Chesapeake, Virginia: Association for the Advancement of Computing Education.

Ludwig-Hardman, S. & Dunlap, J. C. (2003). Learner Support Services for Online Students: Scaffolding for success. *International Review of Research in Open and Distance Learning,* 4(1), 197-211.

McKenzie, O., Christensen, E.L. & Rigby, P.H. (1968). *Correspondence instruction in the United States.* New York: McGraw Hill.

Morrow, J., Phillips, D. & Bethune, E. (2007). Teaching and learning: flexible modes and technology applications. *British Journal of Midwifery, 15*(7), 445-448.

Muirhead, B. & Betz, M. (2005). Transitional Developments in Online Courses and Programs: Theory and Practice. *Educational Technology & Society, 8*(2), 1-6.

Nichols, M. & Gardner, N. (2002). Evaluating flexible delivery across a Tertiary Institution. *Open Learning, 17*(1), 11-22.

Richardson, J.T.E. & Price, L. (2003). Approaches to studying and perceptions of academic quality in electronically delivered courses. *British Journal of Educational Technology, 34*(1), 45-56.

Shih, T.K., Hung, J.C., Ma, J. & Jin, Q. (2007). A Survey of Distance Education Challenges and Technologies. In T.K. Shih and J.C. Hung (Eds.), *Future Directions in Distance Learning and Communication Technologies* (pp.1 -25). London: Information Science Publishing.

Simonson, M., Smaldino, S., Albright, M. & Zvacek, S. (2000). *Teaching and learning at a distance-Foundations of distance education.* New Jersey: Prentice-Hall, Inc.

Simpson, O. (2000). *Open and Distance Learning Series. Supporting Students in Open and Distance Learning.* London: Kogan Page Limited.

Smith, P.J., & Smith, S.N. (1999). Differences between Chinese and Australian students: Some implications for distance educators. *Distance Education, 20*(1), 64-80.

Taylor, J.C. (1995). Distance education technologies: The fourth generation. *Australian Journal of Educational Technology, 11*(2), 1-7.

Taylor, J.C. (2000). New Millennium Distance Education. In V. Reddy and S. Manjulika (Eds.), *The World of Open and Distance Learning* (pp. 475-480). India: Viva Books Private Ltd.

Yorke, M., Bernett, G., Evanson, P., Haines, C., Jenkins, D., Knight, P., Scurry, D., Stowell, M. & Woolf, H. (2005). Mining institutional datasets to support policy making and implementation. *Journal of Higher Education Policy and Management, 27*(2), 285-298.

Zepke, N., Leach, L., Prebble, T., Campbell, A., Coltman, D., Dewart, B., Gibson, M., Henderson, J., Leadbeater, J., Purnell, S., Rowan, L., Solomon, N. & Wilson, S. (2005). *Improving tertiary student outcomes in the first year of study.* Wellington, New Zealand: Teaching and Learning Research Initiative.

Appendix 1: Questionnaire

This research project aims to investigate the learning experience of students studying at Curtin University through flexible delivery mode. All students enrolled in Research and Evaluation in International Health and Topics in International Health are being asked to complete a short questionnaire, prior to the conclusion of Semester Two. The survey should take no more than ten minutes to complete.

Any information will be treated in the strictest confidence. No identifying data will be included in the final report unless the respondent has given permission. All collected information will be carefully secured at all times by the researcher. Raw data will only be accessed by Kate Thomson and research assistants who may be involved in the data analysis. The tutor and unit coordinator will not have access to this data.

http://www.surveymonkey.com/MySurvey_EditPage.aspx?sm=zU4Of-sFMFOsRxjoNeW41ANpD2JKMQxpARrnnDc9UIZxqY9E7%2b%2b-GH1nCQke00aKRd8V8pPdFSZOSpWBIugc4twbhx2xVzg46p6SqxOjG-xz%2bQ%3d&TB_iframe=true&height=475&width=650

*1. Which unit(s) are you enrolled in?[1]

- Research and Evaluation in International Health
- Topics in International Health
- Both REIH and Topics

*2. Are you?

- Male
- Female

*3. How old are you?[2]

*4. Are you an International Student?

- Yes
- No
- I do not know

*5. What culture or ethnicity do you identify with? For example, Asian-Indian or Chinese-Australian.

---

1. Questions marked with an asterisk were compulsory
2. Question 3 allowed a freeform response

*6. Where do you live?

- Australia
- Asia
- Europe
- America
- Africa
- Other (please specify)

*7. What is the highest level of education you have completed?[3]

*8. In which degree are you enrolled?

*9. Are you currently employed?

*10. Would you consider this?

- Full-time
- Part-time
- Casual
- Voluntary
- Other (please specify)

*11. What is your main occupation?[4]

*12. How do you usually access the internet?

- Personal-I have a connection to the internet at home
- Business-I use the computer where I work to access the internet
- Casual-I use Internet cafes, or borrow friends' computers to access the internet
- Other (please specify)

*13. What kind of internet connection is this?

- 28.8Kbps modem
- 56 Kbps modem
- IDSN
- Cable modem
- DSL
- T1 or better
- I do not know
- Other (please specify)

3.Questions 7 and 8 required a response from a drop down menu

4.Question 11 allowed a freeform response

*14. Did you use the Computer Mediated Communication (ie Skype or MSN) offered in this unit?

- Yes
- No

*15A. Please tell us why you chose to use this form of communication; was it to ask about

- Assignment 1
- Assignment 2
- The take home exam
- The readings
- The unit outline
- Referencing
- An extension
- Other (please specify)

*15B. Please explain why you chose not to use this form of communication (you can select as many options as are appropriate for you)

- There is a time difference
- I don't have a camera
- I don't have a microphone
- My internet is too slow
- I was uncomfortable with the technology
- I didn't need to
- Other (please specify)

*17. Please indicate whether you agree or disagree with the following set of statement[5] :

- I believe this communication affected my learning experience in a positive way
- I believe this communication better prepared me for the assignments
- I believe this communication assisted with the learning outcomes of the unit
- I would like this opportunity for communication made available in other units
- I would use additional modes of communication, such as online face-to-face communication via Skype or MSN, if they were available in other units

---

5. These questions required a response using Likert scales, from Strongly Agree to Strongly Disagree, with an N/A option. See Table 2 for detail.

http://www.surveymonkey.com/QuestionBuilderFrame.aspx?sm=zU4Of-sFMFOsRxjoNeW41ANpD2JKMQxpARrnnDc9UIZw5eHdG1%2b-grKvtODqHLofoay9sSBOG%2f%2bwbRWoEhyvbMdVXjnetfyp454-FrHXhosOa8%3d&TB_iframe=true&height=*&width=725

18. Please use the space below to comment on the aspects of this communication that you enjoyed and have helped you learn[6]

19. Please use the space below to recommend improvements to this form of communication

20. Please use the space below for recommendations or suggestions for improving any aspect of your learning experience at Curtin University

21. Are there any other comments you would like to make?

javascript:void(null);http://www.surveymonkey.com/QuestionBuilder-Frame.aspx?sm=zU4OfsFMFOsRxjoNeW41ANpD2JKMQxpARrn-nDc9UIZyQEauknecQ6hN7xVXBSAjoOPZH6w7ltGL%2b89kCZZI-xsmdoQ16%2fov5nraoS9%2fzbOipmuqOEnriqh9QsNL84ImfVpht-3bJr8MLKAKDKmxci6rwNZ7sQRbyH2%2b9f%2foray998%3d&TB_iframe=true&height=*&width=700http://www.surveymonkey.com/MySurvey_EditPage.aspx?sm=zU4OfsFMFOsRxjoNeW41ANpD2JKM-QxpARrnnDc9UIZyQWyQ%2bkfg6bttLAmjLdsZxYEQWSczEmVDv-%2fy%2fpE2wN6og3pBa1ENQVreiQh1R8Y5M%3d&TB_iframe=true-&height=475&width=650

Thank you

Thank you for taking the time to complete this survey. When the research has been completed, you will be provided with a one page summary of results.

If you have any questions or concerns, please do not hesitate to contact those listed on the information sheet.

javascript:void(null);http://www.surveymonkey.com/QuestionBuilder-Frame.aspx?sm=zU4OfsFMFOsRxjoNeW41ANpD2JKMQxpARrnnDc9-UIZxPGFWUBOSscUCzShAf2HZIVJiTu2VTDpE5bgg7lfwxKiDLQO-mUTejqXk4B%2bTF81YYaRtOwZpw9XDQ%2fgEC%2fe/QKy%2f3R-q7yHKm45PsoRogMBEEUwyr1Qg1Np68k4i%2foJPEc%3d&TB_iframe=-true&height=*&width=700http://www.surveymonkey.com/MySurvey_Edit Page.aspx?sm=zU4OfsFMFOsRxjoNeW41ANpD2JKMQxpARrnnDc9-UIZw41uxCZAaGtk7%2flKZ6aHIcYytlS2cH3TvNjySYmxbJ5f1dhNCL6-qnX%2fc%3d&TB_iframe=true&height=475&width=650

6.Questions 18-21 allowed freeform responses

Part II

Learning through Online Communities

Using Technology for Pre-Service Second Language Teacher Education through WebCT (Web Course Tools)

Carmen Pérez Basanta

Introduction

Regarded by many as a major form of advanced distance learning, the University of Granada (Spain) has taken various measures to boost web-based education. This university has established a Centre for Virtual Learning (CEVUG) to take charge of their web-based graduate and postgraduate courses delivered via the educational platform, WebCT, and in 2005 it has also launched an online pre-service teacher education programme.

In the Spanish educational system, becoming a qualified teacher of English requires a university degree and a pre-service course on teaching education leading to a Certificate in Education, entitled "Certificate of Pedagogic Aptitude" (CAP). This postgraduate course consists of 10 credits of general pedagogy and 2.5 of English methodology followed by a three-month supervised teaching practice in a secondary school. If successful, you gain a recognized certificate (CAP) which enables you to teach in a private or state secondary school. So far these teacher training courses have been held on campus and only recently some universities have launched virtual courses for obtaining this accreditation. This paper presents a piloting study to implement English methodology through virtual learning by means of WebCT

(Web Course Tools). It is hoped that this web-based learning will offer: round-the-clock availability, at-home flexibility, self-pacing, cost-effectiveness and increased opportunities for collaborative learning.

What we want to offer in this paper is the pedagogical considerations of the design of this online teacher training course. This course bears upon the teacher training "model" of Michael Wallace (1991) which advocates the role of the teacher as a "reflective practitioner" –someone who reflects on the practice of teaching English as a foreign language. With regard to instructional design, our intention is to produce good and interactive materials to foster students' interest and motivation as well as interactivity and learner autonomy. We also deal with the utilities of the digital platform WebCT. Detailed descriptions of all these aspects are discussed in the following sections.

The Reflective Model, Constructivism and Online Learning For Pre-service Education

Despite the general idea that "technology is driving pedagogy", we decided to challenge this assumption by first establishing the psychopedagogical model and then looking into the best way of delivering it. According to Day (1993) pre-service ESL teacher education falls into two major approaches or models.The first one emphasizes the knowledge base or subject matter we believe our students must acquire. The second model attends to the way in which that knowledge is delivered. Since it is beyond the scope of this paper to describe these models in detail –apprentice-expert model, rationalist model, case studies model and integrative model (Day, 1993)– we will concentrate on an integrative approach, known as the "reflective model" (Wallace, 1991), based upon the work of educational thinkers such as Dewey (1933, cited in Day,1993). Michael Wallace's model (1991) focuses on critical reflection as a cognitive bridge between theory and practice and contends that the proper form of teacher development should be concerned not only with imparting conceptual knowledge but with the cognitive or epistemological status of reflection, as a catalyst to build up real knowledge. By and large, this model tries to arouse critical reasoning about the factors of learning and its adaptation to cope with students' needs and circumstances.

For Wallace (1991), being a "professional" implies two kinds of knowledge: "received knowledge" or the necessary pedagogic content knowledge, and "experiential knowledge" or the professional's ongoing experience. Thus, the first dimension involves the necessary pedagogic content of the profession imparted through lectures, readings, discussions, and so on, while the second one is concerned with procedural knowledge or knowledge-in-action. These two types of knowledge should be further developed by practice (hands-on experience), and the opportunity to reflect on that knowledge in practice (Fig. 1) -it is also possible to develop experiential knowledge by the observation of practice.

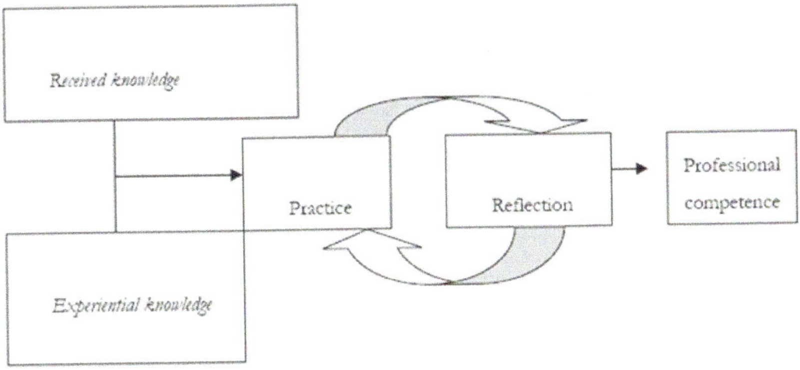

Figure 1: The Reflective Model

Thus the professional knowledge bases are identified on the far left of the diagram, either as received knowledge -facts, data, theories etc.- or experiential knowledge -practical experience (Wallace, 1993). In the centre of the diagram, the trainee acts upon (practice), then reflects on the action, develops hypotheses (reflection) which are tried out in more action (practice). Hence, we can see a cycle of learning, trying out hypotheses, reflecting, and additional action in which the hypotheses are tried out in the classroom. All this leads to the goal of this model: professional competence (on the far right of the diagram).

In fact, this emphasis on active learning in this model is a response to traditional theoretical models which supposedly bring about limited student engagement with course material. We agree with Ur (1992) and Day (1993) that in pre-service teacher training there has been an over-emphasis on the rationalist approach – "learn-the-theory-and-then- apply-it model" (Ur, 1992: 56)– and then there is increasing evidence that it does not help teachers develop professionally.

Another asset of this model is that it shares important principles with constructivism such as: connection between theory and practice, self-awareness, active-learning and an increase emphasis on student-centredness. In this respect, it has been vastly proven that constructivism fits well with virtual learning (Driscoll, 1994). Some even suggest that the come-back of constructivism is due to its obvious affinities with web-based pedagogy.

It is probably no accident that constructivism is gaining popularity and momentum at the same time interactive, user friendly computer technologies are becoming widely available. The computer offers effective means for implementing constructivist strategies that would be difficult to accomplish in other media. (Driscoll, 1994: 376)

I myself have found a close parallel between these two pedagogic lines which could be summarised as follows:

Constructivism	Web-based learning
construction of learning through meaningful activities	authentic and multimedia materials
emphasis on big concepts not hierarchical knowledge	hypertextuality
collaborative learning	WebCT communication tools
coaching and scaffolding	human mediation and interaction
learner's responsibility	distance learning and learner autonomy

Taking on board these constructs, we are firmly convinced that reflective teaching and constructivist views on learning go hand in hand with online learning. And this is the major reason why we have chosen this model.

Course Description of Cap

This course is designed for trainee students who want to gain qualifications in English methodology by means of a short and intensive online course. The course revolves around the notion of "modules". A module can have one or more units or topics, accompanied by activities. This course emphasizes activities rather than theoretical issues, which adopt different formats depending on the degree of interactivity and feedback. There are 8 modules covering a wide range of thematic contents accompanied by a wide range of activities. These activities are of different sorts (assignments, quizzes and self-tests) and have to be completed and submitted online within a limited period of time (approximately 2 weeks per module, totalling 16 weeks). Once students complete the activity, they send them to their instructor and received credit, which is included as a percentage of their grade in the course. The other categories for grading include final exam grades and participation in discussions. Thus, completed activities are counted as part of the final grade together with the final exam mark.

In terms of procedures, students are required to attend an introductory session which brings them into contact with the teacher and their classmates, and a session to take a final online exam held on campus, but the whole of the course is fully-virtual. In terms of communication skills, it should be particularly noted that they are required to log onto online forums at least twice a week with questions or comments. Consultation with the teacher can be done via e-mail, forum or through tutorials on campus.

Methodology

The main objective of this course is to implement a methodology which will develop learners' autonomy through self-access and interactive learning. A growing list of authors (Holec, 1981, 1988; Benson and Voller, 1997; Benson, 2000) are foregrounding the importance of promoting learner autonomy in

ELT. According to Brett (1996), one approach which is particularly well-suited to multimedia is autonomous language learning due to the ease with which it can be adapted to accommodate learners' preferences. Likewise, numerous studies underline the role that the web might play in fostering independent learners (Motteram, 1997; Healy, 2002) as learners have to make their own choices and thus take more responsibility over their own learning.

This leads us to another issue: the importance of learner personal involvement and motivation. We think that online learning has something to offer insofar students can work at their own pace and engage in both short and long-term "discovery" learning tasks (Thorne and Thorne, 2000). This might provide a solid foundation on which to tackle the perennial problem of involving and motivating students as it is widely been acknowledged (Warschauer, 1996c). We should, however, be aware that the provision of technological learning or CALL programmes "per se" do not guarantee success (Warschauer and Healey, 1998). If we want the web to become a worthwhile learning tool, we contend that it should meet the following requirements (Perez Basanta, 2004):

- Learners should be primarily directed to find materials they can understand and learn from. Therefore, activities will require considerable research for the teacher and extensive teacher support.
- Computer-based programmes should be task-orientated so that students have both feasible goals and outcomes. Contrary to this, activities in which the learners' output consists of solely mouse clicks, provide no opportunity for learning (Chapelle, 1997)
- Students need to be engaged with the task and not just surf the web. One of the major hurdles when working with the web is navigation. In this sense, a big fear when using the Internet is that of students scavenging over the World Wide Web.
- We should promote the ability to go from site to site via hypertext with the least effort and time.
- We should use our site as a gateway to other websites, those in EFL and others.
- Materials should be designed to meet students' needs, interests, experiences and expectations. Thus, it is useful to perform a needs analysis.
- To foster interactive learning, there should be a degree of learner support in the form of dictionaries, glossaries, ELT resources etc. so that students are enabled to become more independent.
- Students should have a sense of progress and continuous feedback. If they do not have a feeling of going somewhere, they will soon become demotivated.
- Materials should be produced according to web typographical conventions and layout (length, type-faces, colours, etc).
- All materials should be piloted, tested and updated.

Syllabus Contents

Like any other mode of teaching and learning a language, web-based learning is only worthwhile when it is guided by sound pedagogical principles which are girded up by theoretical notions of language learning and acquisition. The syllabus that follows has therefore been elaborated with a due regard for theory of teaching/learning and the action (or praxis) of the class. In fact, efforts have been made to ensure that it is based on state-of-the-art techniques and on strong and, where appropriate, innovative theoretical considerations. As mentioned before, we very strongly believe that web-based contents should not be technology-driven, but pedagogy-led.

We will first consider the main requirements which surround CALL concerning syllabus design. In terms of devising a syllabus for an online course, we should be fully aware of the primary differences between language learning via the web, as opposed to conventional classroom learning. It is widely acknowledged that distance learning imposes some requirements on syllabus design. One of the most salient is that the syllabus should not be product-based –i.e. a mere list of contents– but process-based – i.e. an inventory of activities (White, 1995). The pedagogical goal of the teaching through ICT is to improve performance by participating in interaction. Here the computer acts as a participant and it can well be argued that our learners work interactively with the computer (Chapelle, 1997). It is also interesting to note that in this activity-based approach learners build up knowledge by engaging in some sort of interaction. In this sense, the pedagogical theory behind web-based learning is constructivism (Zahorik, 1995).

Nevertheless, the afore-mentioned performance-based approach does not seem to be contradictory with the idea of having content aims in mind. In fact, after considering current thinking on English methodology, we set out the following objectives which provide direction for the construction of the modules:

MODULE 1: A THEORY OF LANGUAGE TEACHING: TEACHING BY PRINCIPLES

- Cognitive principles:
  - Automaticity.
  - Meaningful learning.
  - Anticipation of reward or extrinsic motivation.
  - Intrinsic motivation: "Ten commandments for motivating language learners".
  - Strategic investment: learner strategies.
  - Summary of language strategies.

- Affective principles:
  - Language ego.
  - Self-confidence.
  - Risk-taking.
  - The language culture connection.

- Linguistic principles:
  - The native language effect.
  - Interlanguage.
  - Communicative language competence.

MODULE 2: LISTENING

- Cognitive processes in L2 listening: implications for teaching and learning.
- Implications for the classroom.
- Listening skills.
- Stages of listening: listening activities.
- Using video as a way of developing listening.
- Prerequisite conditions: some basic criteria of "good video".
- The video lesson plan: some techniques.
- General principles for listening or watching videos.

MODULE 3: READING

- The nature of reading: what is reading?
- Reading purposes.
- What makes a text difficult?
- Intensive and intensive reading.
- Selecting a text.
- Exploitation of texts: stages of reading.
- Reading skills or strategies: bottom-up and top-down.
- Typology of reading activities.

MODULE 4: SPEAKING

- The nature of oral communication.
- Components of speaking.
- Problems in learning speaking.
- New techniques to teach oral English.
  - Controlled activities.
  - Awareness activities.
  - Fluency activities.
  - Feedback activities.
- Stages to setting up feedback tasks.
- Guidelines for promoting speaking in the classroom.

MODULE 5: WRITING

- What's writing?
- What do we write?
- Speech and writing
- Why writing is difficult?
- Why teach writing?
- Learning to use the resources of the written language.
- The writer's product and process.
- Writing approaches in the classroom.
- The role of guidance.
- Approaches to teaching writing:
    - The controlled or reinforcement approach.
    - The paragraph-pattern approach or model writing.
    - The communicative approach.
    - The process approach or free writing.
- Correcting written work.

MODULE 6: THE CURRICULUM FOR FLUENCY IN SPANISH SECONDARY EDUCATION

- Introduction.
- Aims and objectives
- Syllabus contents:
    - Linguistic contents.
    - Pragmatic and sociolinguistic contents.
    - Skill contents.
    - Discoursal competence.
- Methodology.
- Evaluation.

MODULE 7: LESSON PLANNING

- Class.
- Textbook.
- Level.
- Length of lesson.
- Aims or objectives.
- Anticipated problems.
- Activities/tasks or exercises.
- Homework.
- Materials.
- Evaluation.

MODULE 8: TESTING

- Definition of testing.
- Purposes of testing.
- Types of tests.
- Qualities of a good test: validity and reliability.
- Testing methods.
- Classroom or progress tests: stages and design.

For the delivery of these contents we have made use of the devices described in the next section.

Activities

One of the big issues for the support and delivery of activities should be organised around the concept of 'interactivity'. As Brennan et al. (2000, internet) state:

This term can be used to refer to levels of engagement with computer based learning resources, everything from sitting and receiving information and activities with the learner ostensibly in 'control'; through to collaborative relationships with others Online in a constructed environment where the learner pursues interests and ideas with some scaffolding of support.

To us, WebCT is the best provider of interactivity. Firstly, it gives feedback to students by means of three different activities: assignments, self-tests and quizzes. Assignments are Word documents which the learner downloads from the platform to be completed and sent via WebCT to be corrected and marked by the teacher. Quizzes are usually automatically corrected by the platform, and the results can be consulted both by the teacher and the student. Self-tests are tests which can be taken an unlimited number of times until you get the right answer, or some other kind of feedback. Apart from these devices, we have hyperlinked others resources to facilitate self-study. In this regard we can name the following techniques: 3. Interactive examples for illustrating a point you are making. 4. Further explanations for providing additional information or expand upon a matter of some complexity. 5. Obligatory readings, where theoretical developments are offered. 6. Warnings or teaching tips about potential problems. 7. Diagrams and summaries for giving short and orderly accounts about important points.

In sum, all these activities are aimed at promoting interactivity, autonomy and monitoring, and are signalled by visual icons.

WebCT Communication Tools

Due to space constraints we cannot give full consideration to WebCT tools (glossary, calendar, grade management, progress tracking and management, evaluation surveys, online quizzes and assignments, chat tool, e-mail, forums, etc.) but it is well-recognised that WebCT contributes to:

- Create, maintain, and add course materials interactively through the web.
- Integrate multimedia.
- Design web-pages with different formats (including images, movies, sound).
- Provide communication tools –email, discussions, chats, whiteboard– for collaborative and social learning.
- Assess student performance during the course (quizzes, surveys and assignments).
- Break the barriers of space and time through distance learning and learning autonomy.

It is particularly noteworthy the promotion of interactivity by means of communication tools. In fact, WebCT provides the assistance of computer-mediated communication (CMC) for replicating the interactions of the classrooms. E-mails, discussion forums, chats and whiteboards are beginning to offer a new environment for interaction between student-teacher, student-student(s) and teacher-student(s) in an asynchronous or synchronous way. Research work is just beginning to establish the implications of this form of online support but it is our experience and belief that CMC is highly beneficial and in next section will provide some evidence.

The Study: Assessing the Course through a Questionaire

Although it has become a truism to talk about the benefits of online learning, there has been very little research on virtual learning (Stepp-Greany, 2002). There is urgent need to carry out both quantitative and qualitative measures for assessing students' outcomes. Here we are going to report on a descriptive study of student perceptions about the use of main components of this course. Drawing on Stepp-Greany (2002), we designed a questionnaire of 20 questions with different formats –Likert scales, nominal and open questions. For the purposes of this article, data are reported in numbers and percentages of student responses for each statement. The statements are ordered from those receiving the highest number to the lowest number of responses. Due to space constraints we will only show the results of 10 questions we have considered most relevant and illuminating. It was administered to 13 students and its main objective was to know the perceptions of students towards the following questions:

a. The role of the teacher in an online environment.
b. Planning and effectiveness of the programme and activities.
c. Comparison between traditional learning and online learning.
d. Motivation and technical difficulty.
e. The value of communication tools.

Results and Discussion

Question 1: In comparison with traditional leaning, relationship with the teacher was:

Much closer	*Closer*	*The same*	*Less close*	*More distant*

Over three quarters of students (8.46) highly valued the relationship with the teacher, rejecting the fallacy that virtual learning is a solitary activity. This clearly indicates that students felt that there was a close interaction between teacher-students. Certainly we can easily infer that a good rapport was achieved.

RELATIONSHIP WITH TEACHER	Frequency	Percentage
-much closer	*3*	*23.1*
-closer	*8*	*61.5*
-less close	*2*	*15.4*
TOTAL	*13*	*100*

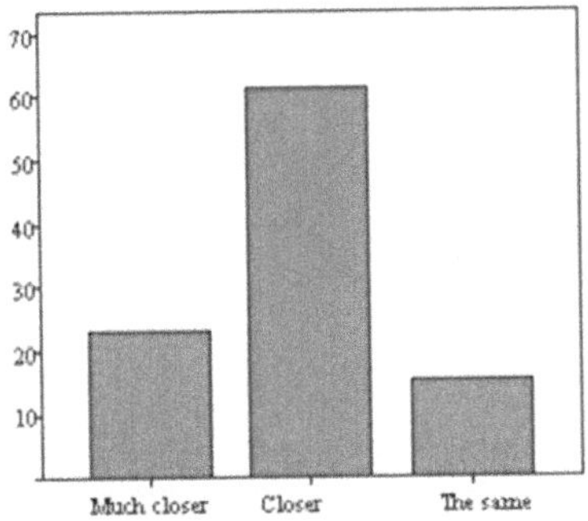

Question 2: Feedback and assistance from the teacher through online discussions and emails was:

Of much help	Of help	Of some help	Of little help	Of no help

The answer to this question is crucial since it explains the role of the teacher in an online environment, obviously facilitated by WEbCT communication tools. A majority of students (69.2) agreed that feedback and assistance from the teacher through online discussions was of much help. This perception is in line with findings by other researchers (Kern, 1996) McGrath, 1998); according to Stepp-Greanny's study the teacher's role is significant in technology-mediated instruction. This also implies the usefulness of WebCT communications tools which facilitate interaction.

Feedback and assistance from teacher through online discussions and emails	Frequency	Percentage
–of much help	9	69.2
–of help	4	30.8
Total	13	100.0

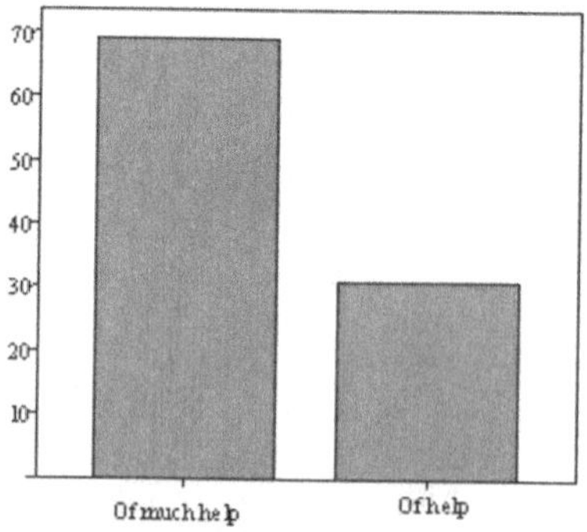

Question 3: In comparison with traditional teaching, planning was:

Much better	*Better*	*The same*	*Worse*	*Much worse*

Here there is almost a unanimous consensus (86.0) that web-based planning was more effective in virtual learning than in traditional learning. We are firmly convinced that WebCT tools -the use of calendars, glossaries, students' tips, interactivity from quizzes and assignments, marks, etc.- facilitated and contributed to manage learning in a more organised and effective way. Students know what their objectives are, they are permanently assisted through interactive activities and human mediation can make use of resources within and out of the platform that guide their ongoing progress and ultimately collect permanent feedback on their performance.

PLANNING IN VIRTUAL LEARNING	Frecuencia	Percentage
– much better	4	30,8
– better	6	46,2
– the same	3	23,1
Total	13	100,0

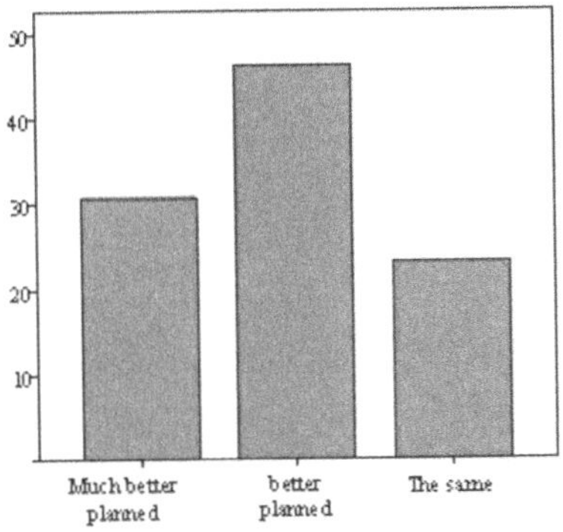

Question 4: Choose the activities you think are the most useful:

Quizzes	*Assignments*	*Summaries*	*Further readings*	*Examples*	*Diagrams*

We wished to know which activities with different degrees of interactivity (assignments, quizzes, examples, readings, further explanations, summaries and diagrams) were more helpful. Results confirmed that assignments, which you download, complete and upload to be corrected and graded by the teacher, were the favourites (53.8%), followed by quizzes and examples with an equal result (32.1). The reason was perhaps that assignments are more creative –their answers are open- contrary quizzes and self-tests which are in the majority of cases multiple-choice questions.

USEFULNESS OF ACTIVITIES	Frequency	Percentage
–quizzes	3	23.1
–assignments	7	53.8
– examples	3	23.1
Total	13	100.0

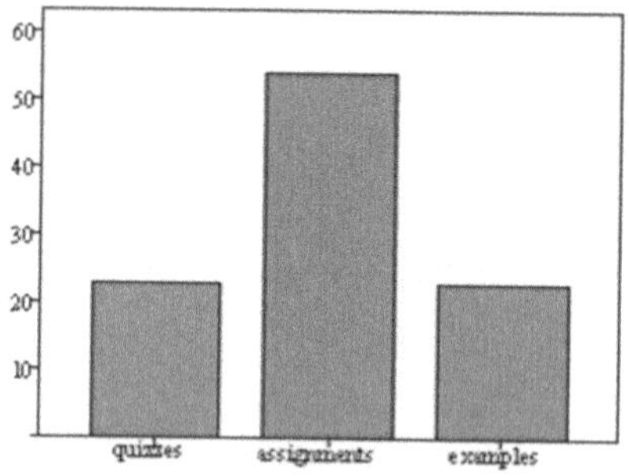

Question 5: When you had a problem, how did you solve it:

With the assistance of the teacher	With the assistance of a classmate	With the assistance of the teacher and classmate	I half solved it	I didn' t solve it

It is particularly remarkable that students solved their problems not only with the assistance of the teacher (23.1) but with the help of the teacher and other students (72.2). As shown in the online discussions, there was a constant stream of information between teacher/student(s) which undoubtedly led to the resolution of problems.

SOLVING PROBLEMS	Frequency	Percentage
– with the teacher's assistance	3	23.1
–with the teacher's and classmate's assistance	10	72.2
Total	13	100.0

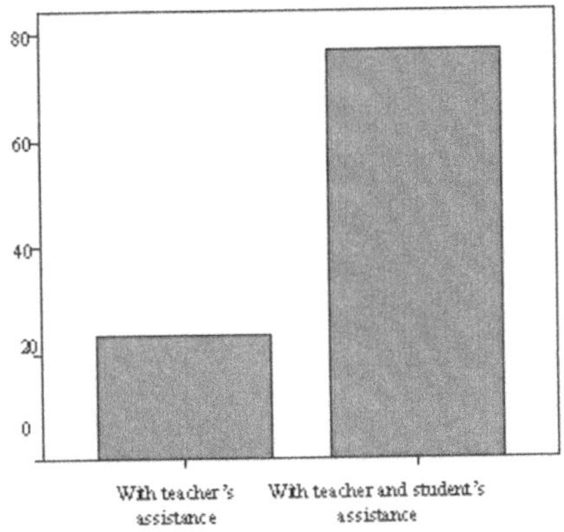

Question 6: In comparison with traditional learning, do you think that you have invested:

Much more time	More time	The same	Less	Much less

Almost 69% of the students felt that they invested more time on the technology-enhanced course than in a regular in-the-ground course. Slightly over 30% felt that time investment was the same. This is a positive factor since there is a strong agreement that time on task is a learning benefit, and according to Stepp-Greany (2002) "it is frequently cited as a factor in achievement". Here our results coincide with Stepp-Greany in the sense that web-based courses are more time-consuming than traditional courses. Again this contradicts the popular assumption that online learning is less demanding.

TIME INVESTMENT	Frequency	Percentage
– much more	4	30.8
– more	5	38.5
– the same	4	30.8
Total	13	100.0

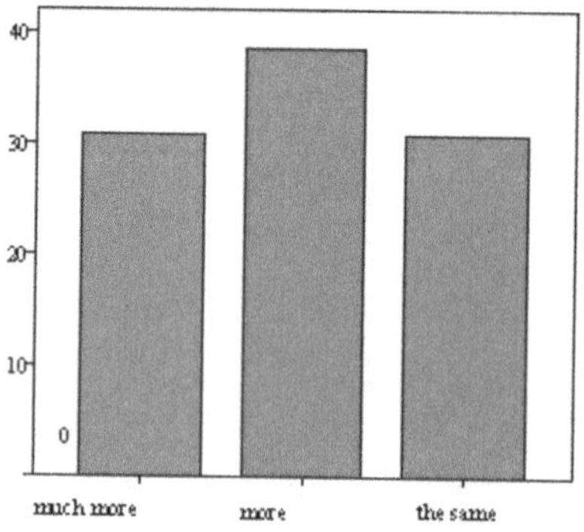

Question 7: Rank these types of learning according to what you consider it was more promoted in this course:

- Conceptual knowledge.
- Practice.
- Critical learning.
- Reflection.
- Materials design.
- Evaluation.
- Discovery learning.
- Rote learning.

According to the psychopedagogical model (reflective model and constructivism) we drew upon for the design of this course, it was predictable that the most elected types of learning were: practice followed by reflection and critical learning, and it was very encouraging to see that rote learning was the last option. As mentioned before, the aims of this course were to enhance constructivist paradigms so that instead of students being passive recipients of knowledge they actively participate in the construction of new knowledge through hands-on activities, reflection and critical learning. Therefore we strongly believe that our pedagogical objectives were fulfilled.

Assessemnent of Learning	1st	2nd	3rd	4th	5th	6th	7th	8th
Conceptual learning	7.7	23.1	7.7	7.7	23.1	30.8	15.4	7.7
Practice	30.8	7.7	46.2	7.7	23.1	7.7	7.7	7.7
Critical learning	23.1	23.1	7.7	23.1		15.4	7.7	
Reflection	15.4	30.8	23.1	15.4	7.7			15.4
Materials Design	7.7	7.7	15.4	7.7		23.1		30.8
Evaluation	7.7	7.7	23.1	15.4	23.1	7.7	53.8	15.4
Discovery learning	7.7	7.7		23.1	23.1	15.4	7.7	
Rote learning			15.4		7.7	7.7	7.7	84.6
TOTAL	100.0	100.0	100.0	100.0	100.0	100.0	100.0	100.0

Question 8: If you compare this online course with traditional learning, would you consider it:

Much more motivating	More motivading	The same	Less motivating	Boring

Undoubtedly, one of the factors more investigated in e-learning has been motivation. As aforementioned, Warschauer (1996a; 1996b; 1996c) has vastly proven that it is a very motivating factor. The results of this questionnaire confirmed this assumption. Over 84% supported that computer-mediated learning was more motivating than face to face instruction in regular classes.

TRADICIONAL VS. VIRTUAL LEARNING MOTIVATION	Frequency	Percentage
– Much more	1	7.7
– More	11	84.6
– The same	1	7.7
Total	13	100.0

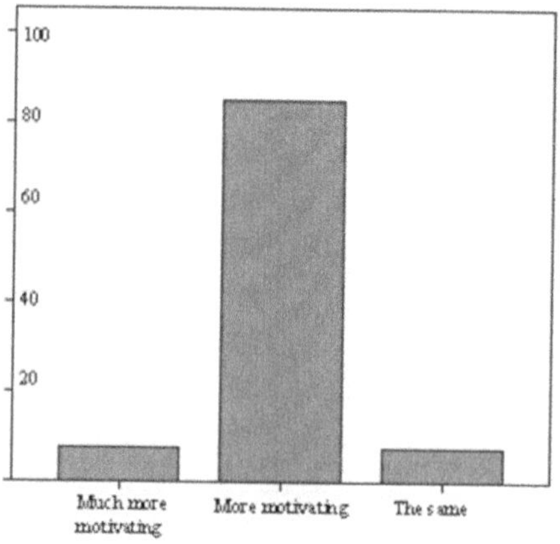

Question 9: How many times have you logged onto online discussions?

More than four times	Three times	Twice	Once	Rarely

Discussions or forums promote student-to-student and students-to-teacher communication around topics and questions relative to your course. The advantage of discussion over email is that postings can be easily arranged into topics and threads. Thus, when you enter the discussions area, you will see different topics corresponding to the different modules, listed in the same way you use file folders to organize papers. Hence, discussions are organized in a sequence of messages related to each other (known as threaded discussions). Discussions can be used in many ways e.g. to comment on module points, to ask for assistance, to discuss assignments, or just to get to know other students on your course, etc. but their ultimate objective is to promote linguistic interactivity and social learning.

Although there seems to be a dearth of data on the use of discussions and emails, there are compelling reasons to believe the important effect of these communication tools on instruction and interaction in foreign language.

As far as this study was concerned, it should be highlighted that students made a good use of online discussions, 61% logged in more than 4 times a week whereas only 7.7% stuck to the course regulations logging in twice a week with an odd case who posted one message a week.

DISCUSSION POSTINGS	Frequency	Percentage
– more than tour	8	61.1
– three times	1	7.7
– twice	3	23.1
– once	1	7.7
Total	13	100.0

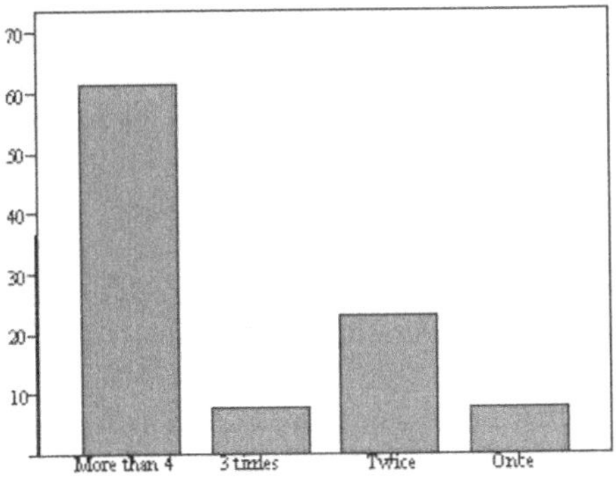

Question 10: Communication through discussions was:

Very interesting	Interesesting	So so	Ocassionally interesting	Useless

With this question we really wanted to elicit from students their opinions about the usefulness of discussions and whether they raised interest and expectation. Their opinions were almost unanimous: 38.5% found very interesting and 61.5 interesting. To our mind, a good use of the discussions is essential for enhancing feedback and interactivity among teacher-student and student-teacher. Again, it should be noted here that for a good functioning of online discussions teachers should provide students with some instructions for writing efficient messages, create different topics around particular subjects, develop reciprocity and cooperation among students, and above all give prompt feedback.

INTEREST OF ONLINE DISCUSSIONS	Frequency	Percentage
–very interesting	5	38.5
– interesting	8	61.5
Total	13	100.0

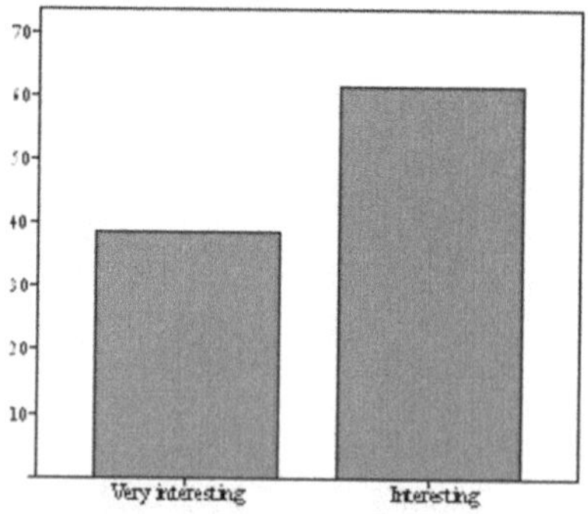

In sum, findings from this small-scale study provide support for the conclusion that they had a successful virtual learning experience. Moreover, students were provided with technological tools (WebCT) that they could use to develop skills necessary for success. At the same time, online learning helped students to increase their motivation by assigning them an active role in taking charge of their own learning. Finally interacting with other students, the teacher, and other course resources led to cooperative and social work.

Nevertheless, a final note should be added in terms of our limitations. Although the results of this study cannot be generalisable due to the small number of students, we believe that it can be used as a starting point for further replication in studies of a similar nature. In this respect, and limited as this research may be, to repeat this study with other learners might shed new light on the usefulness of online learning education.

Conclusion

With the emergence of New Technologies in education, new paths have been opened to alternative ways of providing access to instruction at all levels -primary, secondary and postgraduate. This new revolution is offering academic institutions with a more flexible and open learning environment for postgraduate courses as well as pre-service teacher instruction. Thus the use of technology as a tool for promoting online pre-service instruction at the University of Granada is the focus of this paper. Firstly, we consider the adoption of the psychopedagogical model of Michael Wallace (1991), "the reflective model" based on the fundamental premise that the best way of teacher development should be concerned with reflection and practice as a trigger to build up real knowledge. The second part is devoted to the description of the instructional design of this online modular course (syllabus, activities, WebCT tools, etc.) establishing some principles for effective online learning in terms of the development of autonomy, feedback and interaction. Finally, we report on the results of a research study based on a questionnaire to obtain information on student's perceptions to virtual learning. In this study students report: a) the important role of the teacher in virtual; b) better planning and effectiveness in web-based education than in-the-ground education; c) more time invested into virtual learning than into traditional teaching; d) satisfaction with constructive technology, feedback and motivation; and e) the usefulness of WebCT asynchronous tools for promoting communication and assistance.

References

Basanta, P. (2004). Pedagogic aspects of the design and content of an online course for the development of lexical competence: ADELEX. 16(1)128-149.

Benson, P. and Voller, P. (1997). *Autonomy and Independence in Language Learning*. London: Longman.

Benson, P. (2000). "Autonomy and information technology in the educational discourse of the information age". Presented at *ILEC Conference*, University of Hong Kong.

Brennan, R, McFadden, M. and Law, E. (2001). *All that glitters is not gold: Online Delivery of Education & Training.* Leabrook: NCVER. Retrieved 5 April 2006 from http://www.ncver.edu.au/publications/662.html

Brett, P. (1998). "Using multimedia: A descriptive investigation of incidental language learning". *Computer Assisted Language Learning,* 11/2: 179-200.

Chapelle, C. A. (1997). "CALL in the year 2000: Still in search of research paradigms?". *LLT,* 1/1: 19-43. Retrieved 4 May 2006 from http://llt.msu.edu/vol1num1/chapelle/default.html

Day, R. (1993)."Models and the Knowledge Base of Second Language." *University of Hawai'i Working Papers in ESL*, 11/2: 1-13.

Driscoll, M. (1994). *Psychology of learning for instruction*. Massachusetts, USA: Allyn & Bacon.

Healy, D. (2002). 'Learner Autonomy with Technology: What do language learners need to be successful?' TESOL 2002 CALL-IS Academic Session. Retrieved 4 May 2005 from http://oregonstate.edu/ ~healeyd/tesol2002/autonomy.html

Holec, H. (1981). Autonomy and Foreign Language Learning. Oxford: Pergamon. Holec, H., ed. 1988. Autonomy and Self-directed Learning: Present Fields of Application, Strasbourg: Council of Europe.

Kern, R. (1996). "Computer-mediated communication: Using E-mail exchanges to explore personal histories in two cultures. In M. Warschauer (ed.), *Telecollaboration in foreign language learning: Proceedings of the Hawai'i symposium"* Honolulu: University of Hawai'i, Second Language Teaching & Curriculum Center, 105-109

McGrath, B.(1998). "Partners in learning: twelve ways technology changes the teacher-student relationship". *Technological Horizon in Education*, 25/9: 58-62.

Motteram, G. (1997). "Learner Autonomy and the Web". In V. Darleguy et al. (eds.) *Educational Technology in Language Learning: Theoretical Considerations and Practical Applications*. Lyon, France: INSA (National Institute of Applied Science.

Pérez Basanta, C. (2004). "Pedagogic aspects of the design and content of an online course for the development of lexical competence: ADELEX". *ReCALL* 16/1: 129- 149.

Stepp-Greany, J. (2002). "Student Perceptions on Language Learning in a Technological Environment: Implications for the new Millennium". *LLT*, 6/1: 165-180. Retrieved 23 August 2002 from http://llt.msu.edu/vol6num1/pdf/steppgreany.pdf].

Thorne A. and Thorne, C. (2000). "Building bridges on the Web: Using the Internet for cultural studies". In P. Brett, P. and G. Motteram (eds.), *A Special Interest in Computers: Learning and Teaching with Information and Communications Technologies*. Whitsable, Kent: IATEFL, 59-73.

Ur, P. (1992). "Teacher learning". *ELT Journal* 46/1: 56-61.

Wallace, M. J. (1991). *Training Foreign Language Teachers*. Cambridge: Cambridge University Press.

Warschauer, M. (1996a). "Comparing face-to- face and electronic communication in the second language classroom". *CALICO Journal*, 13/ 2: 7-26.

Warschauer, M. (1996b). *Computer-Mediated Collaborative Learning: Theory and Practice* (Research Note No. 17). University of Hawai'i, Second Language Teaching and Curriculum Center.

Warschauer, M.(1996c). "Motivational aspects of using computers for writing and communication". In M. Warschauer (Ed.), *Telecollaboration in Foreign Language Learning: Proceedings of the Hawai'i Symposium*. Honolulu, HI: University of Hawai'i, Second Language Teaching and Curriculum Center, 29-46.

Warschauer, M. and Healey, D. (1998). "Computers and language learning: An overview". *Language Teaching*, 31: 57-71.

White, R.V. (1995). *The ELT Curriculum*. Oxford: Blackwell.

Zahorik, J.A. (1995). *Constructivist Teaching*. Bloomington, IN.: Phi Delta Kappa Educational Foundation.

Lurking and Learning

A Study of Vicarious Interaction in the Online Classroom

Mark Mabrito

Much of the literature in online learning promotes the idea that successful online learning must provide an "interactive" experience for students. Indeed, many studies have confirmed that students perform better academically and rate courses higher that feature some form of interaction (Fulford & Zhang, 1993). Swan (2001) cited "a constructive and dynamic discussion between students and peers" as one of three factors which contribute to the success of asynchronous online courses. The quantity and quality of instructor interactions with students, interactions among students through online discussions, and the value instructors place on these interactions have been linked to student learning (Jiang & Ting, 2000).

In this spirit, the American Distance Education Consortium (ADEC) lists 10 key characteristics of Web-based teaching and learning:

1. Fosters meaning-making, discourse
2. Moves from knowledge transmission to learner-controlled systems
3. Provides for reciprocal teaching
4. Is learner-centered
5. Encourages active participation, knowledge construction
6. Based on higher level thinking skills -- analysis, synthesis, and evaluation
7. Promotes active learning
8. Allows group collaboration and cooperative learning
9. Provides multiple levels of interaction
10. Focuses on real-world, problem solving ("American," 2005).

Although number 9 makes explicit reference to providing interaction in online courses, the remaining points also indirectly speak to the notion of interaction in the online environment. Similarly, the Western Cooperative for Educational Telecommunications in its *Best Practices*, a document supported by the eight major accrediting agencies in this country, lists as one of its guidelines "the importance of appropriate interaction (synchronous or asynchronous) between the instructor and students and among students is reflected in the design of the programs and its courses, and in the technical facilities and services provided" (Best, 2001)

Interaction in the Online Classroom

Clearly, some form of interaction among students and instructor should be the staple of any online learning experience. Interaction in a course can manifest itself in a multiplicity of ways (Mabrito, 2004). Although we typically think of interaction as occurring among students and instructor, students also interact with the design of the course itself and the technology that is used to deliver the course to them. How to promote interaction among students is a topic that receives a great deal of attention in the literature (Moore, 1992; Su, Bonk, Magjuka, Liu, & Lee, 2005). One reason why may be that our current models of interaction in online courses are based heavily on social constructivist theories (see, for example, Hewett & Ehmann, 2004; Lapadat, 2002) that view the online environment as a place where the role of instructor as provider of knowledge is downplayed; rather, social constructivists recognize that knowledge is created as a result of the interactions of members within the course. Social constructivists believe that learning occurs through dialog and shared experiences (Hewett & Ehmann, 2004; Jonassen, Davidson, Collins, Campbell, & Haag, 1995). In the classroom, these experiences involve students interacting with each other and the instructor. Palloff and Pratt (1999) argue that at the heart of successful learning "are the interactions among students themselves, the interactions between faculty and students, and the collaboration in learning that results from these interactions" (p. 5). Jakupcak and Fishbaugh (1998) suggest that anywhere from one-half to one-third of class time should be devoted to encouraging interactive experiences. Similarly, Bull, Kimball, and Stansberry (1998) found that learning is more effective in an online course if there is interaction among learners. Irani (1998) found that with increased interaction came an increase in students' satisfaction and positive outcome in the course.

While consensus seemingly exists in the literature about the importance of interaction in the online classroom, opinion differs as to how interaction should manifest itself. Northrup (2002) argues that interaction should replicate a physical meeting, giving students the comfort of face-to-face meetings; however, attempts to create too much interaction may run the risk of providing too much superfluous activity to students. Anderson and Garrison (1995) studied the effects of two different design groups using the same technology for communication; one group looked at the learners as members of a community where interaction was important while the second group viewed students as independent learners where interaction wasn't important. Students in the group where interaction was considered more important reported more positive experiences.

Whichever approach one may favor, the common assumption is students need to be working and communicating with other students and/or the instructor for successful, meaningful interaction to occur. However, as those of us who have taught in online environments intuitively know, not all students will rise to this challenge. Indeed, some may be lurkers and never become a part of the classroom dynamics. Are these students doomed to become "non-learners" and not reap the same pedagogical benefit from the classroom experience? Or is it possible that some students could have a meaningful, interactive experience apart from directly interacting with other learners?

Sutton (2001) proposes the idea that not all students can effectively participate in interactive classroom experiences. For example, students may not feel comfortable socially or suffer from communication anxiety. Yet, these students may still benefit from observing the interactions of other students or students with the instructor. Specifically, Sutton (2001) defines vicarious learning as "when a student actively observes and processes both sides of direct interaction between another student or between another student and the instructor. Interaction in this sense is not first hand, but one level removed, hence the term vicarious" (p. 227). She further states that students who participate vicariously "can enjoy benefits that are essentially equivalent to those achieved by direct interactors" (p. 232).

While much attention has focused on studying and improving the ways students can participate as "direct interactors" in online environments, very little research has addressed if there might be some pedagogical benefit to building opportunities for vicarious interaction into an online course, if students would view vicarious interaction as positively as direct interaction, or how students might behave when participating vicariously.

A Study of Vicarious and Direct Interaction in an Online Classroom

The purpose of this study was to compare the online experiences of two groups of students in the same class participating both vicariously (by observing the interactions of other students) and as direct interactors (participating in direct, asynchronous conversations with other students) while working on a class project. The following questions were considered:

1. Would levels of participation differ when students participated both vicariously and directly (as direct interactors) while working on a class project?

2. When knowledge gained from vicarious or direct interactions was used as the basis for a subsequent writing assignment, would those assignments differ in length and focus?
3. Would students report different attitudes toward participating in the two different environments?

Design

A case-study approach was used. The students participating in this study were 17 junior- and senior-level college students enrolled in a business writing course. These 9 men and 8 women reported prior experience with using both synchronous and asynchronous online communication; nine of the students had previously completed online courses where some form of online discussion was featured. Students' mean age was 23.2.

Results presented here were gathered from two class units in the course that focused on two different writing projects, similar in nature. The project involved writing an individual report that synthesized the group discussion of a case. For this assignment, the class was split into two groups of fairly equal numbers of men and women. The first group was granted access to an asynchronous discussion board where they could contribute messages and read the messages of other students in the group. The second group was granted access to the same discussion board, but lacked the ability to participate; thus, the second group only could observe the discussion. Additionally, when students read messages in the class discussion area, other students had no way of knowing that they had been present. The discussion board was active for eight days.

For the second assignment, the same procedure was followed with a similar case and for the same length of time, except this time the groups were switched. The students that had interacted with one another the first time (direct interactors) now only could observe the interactions of the other group (participating vicariously). Regardless of how they participated, all students were given the task of writing an analysis of the case based on the collective discussions of the group after each session. Additionally, at the end of each session, students completed a brief survey soliciting their attitudes towards participating in the sessions, as both direct interactors and vicarious participants.

When meeting for asynchronous class discussions, students used the discussion feature provided with WebCT/Vista™. In order to determine how frequently students participated either vicariously or as direct interactors, transcripts from all sessions were saved and analyzed. A word count was performed for each session in which students participated. The courseware program was able to keep a record of how many times students entered each session, how many messages they read, and how many messages they posted to the discussion. The individual written assignments that students completed at the end of each session were collected along with student responses to the survey.

Data Analysis

To analyze conversations that occurred in the asynchronous discussion forums, two independent raters analyzed the transcripts; inter-rater reliability was 84%. In order to quantify the amount of discussion, raters first segmented the discussions into idea units (Loban 1976; Mabrito 2006). A idea unit, as defined by Loban (1976), is "an independent clause with its modifiers" (p. 4). For example, "I'm not sure I would take that approach for that reason" is an example of a single idea unit. Additionally, idea units were categorized as either topic (initiating a new topic of discussion) or comment (a comment or reply to a previous statement).

For each of the two sessions, the total number of idea units read by each student was recorded. At the conclusion of each session, students were asked to complete a written report that presented their understanding of the case analysis. No specific word length or format was specified for this assignment. These assignments also were subjected to the same scale as above—that is, responses were categorized by idea units and whether the units were topics or comments.

Finally, students also completed a brief survey to determine their attitudes toward each of the discussion sessions; responses were measured on a 5-point Likert-type scale.

Results and Discussion

Some interesting patterns were observed as a result of the idea unit analysis. As we can see by Table 1, during sessions when students participated directly with one another, these conversations generated a total of 6,495 idea units. Since during vicarious sessions, students were unable to post messages, there is no comparative total here. However, when comparing the number of idea units read by participants (regardless of whether they were able to contribute or not), those students who were participating vicariously in the sessions read a greater number of idea units (M= 417) than those read by students who actually were participating in the group conversation and generating the idea units (M= 287). Thus, during direct interaction sessions, students contributed more conversation (M= 380) than they spent time reading the conversation of other students (M= 287).

Table 1: Levels of Participation in Asynchronous Discussion Sessions

	Direct Interaction	Vicarious
Total Number of Idea Units Posted to Discussion Board	6465	
Mean =	380	NA
Total Number of Idea Units Read in Discussion Board	4879	7089*
Mean =	287	417

*Note: Total messages read is higher than total posted because students read some messages more than once.

Another question to be addressed during these direct interaction sessions, is what percentage of the conversation was devoted to producing new topics of conversation as compared to responding to the ideas of other students. As we can see in Table 2, when idea units were categorized as either a topic (one that generated a new topic of conversation) or a comment (a reply or follow-up to an existing topic of conversation), during direct interaction sessions, students focused a greater percentage of idea units on generating new topics of conversation (68%) than they did on responding to ideas previously developed by members of the group (32%). These percentages are not surprising, since students contributed more idea units to the conversation than they read. However, online, asynschronous discussions usually follow an opposite pattern, producing more threaded conversations and thus a greater number of topics than comments (Herring, 1999). Generally, in asynschronous discussions, individual topics receive more follow-up comments because participants have more time to consider and respond to topics when working in a non-real-time environment. But asynchronous conversational patterns generally are compared to synchronous or real-time ones (see, for example, Honeycutt, 2001). Here the comparison was between asynchronous involving direct interaction and asynchronous involving vicarious interaction. In this particular instance, when students were directly interacting with one another, they focused more time on contributing to the discussion than they did framing these contributions in the context of what had previously been discussed. When participating vicariously in an asynchronous environment, students were unable to participate, but spent a greater amount of time reading and considering the ideas of other students.

Table 2: Percentage of Topics Versus Comments in Interactive Sessions

	Topics	Comments
Mean Percentage of Idea Units	68%	32%

Just as important a consideration was not only that students spent more time reading the conversation of other students in vicarious sessions as opposed to sessions where they could interact directly, but how their follow-up writing assignments integrated and incorporated the ideas from these two different sessions. The same method of analysis applied to the group conversations also was applied to students' individual writing assignments. As illustrated in Table 3, writing assignments created after sessions of direct interaction produced a total of 2867 idea units (M= 169). Those writing assignments created after vicarious sessions produced a total of 4987 idea units (M= 293). Therefore, writing assignments that followed vicarious sessions, sessions where students read more idea units than in direct interaction sessions, themselves were on average almost twice the length of writing assignments that followed sessions with direct interaction. Students spent more time in vicarious sessions reading the conversations of other students, and this phenomenon may have had some influence on the length of subsequent writing assignments here.

Table 3: Analysis of Idea Units in Subsequent Writing Assignments: Direct Interaction Versus Vicarious

	Direct Interaction	**Vicarious**
Total Number of Idea Units	2867	4987
Mean =	169	293

Although students wrote longer assignments subsequent to vicarious sessions, perhaps more importantly was the question as to what extent students incorporated ideas from the group conversations into these writing assignments. Thus, the idea units in writing assignments also were categorized by topics and comments. A "topic" in this context referred to an original idea not mentioned in the group conversation while a "comment" referred to a follow-up statement to an idea unit or summary of an idea unit presented in the group conversation. As we can see by Table 4, students devoted more time (as indicated by the count of idea units) to referencing group conversations in writing assignments subsequent to vicarious sessions (36% topics versus 64% comments) than they did after sessions with direct interaction (61% topics versus 69% comments). Students had access to both sets of group conversations (when they were interacting directly or vicariously), yet they incorporated more of the ideas culled from sessions where they were not participating than they did from those sessions where they were active participants.

Table 4: Percentage of Topics Versus Comments in Subsequent Writing Assignments: Direct Interaction Versus Vicarious

	Direct Interaction	**Vicarious**
Mean Percentage of Idea Units		
Topics	61%	36%
Comments	39%	64%

The last research question to address was how students perceived the two sessions. Overall, students perceived that working vicariously was more productive (Q1: SA = 10; A = 4) than working interactively (SA = 3; A = 5), as reflected in Table 5. Although they felt more productive in the vicarious sessions, students further perceived that the interactive sessions provided more guidance for completing the writing assignment (Q2: SA = 6; A = 9) than the vicarious sessions (SA = 2; A = 4). On the one hand, when they didn't have to interact with each other, students reported being more productive, yet when they did interact with each other, students reported receiving guidance for completing the assignment. Apparently, being directly involved with the group gave students a better sense of how to proceed with the writing assignment, but not having to be a part of a group gave them a greater sense of productivity when actually producing the writing assignment.

Similarly, students felt they learned more about their topic through interactive sessions (Q3: SA = 7; A = 7) than they did exploring it vicariously (SA = 4; A = 4). As we can see, students acknowledged that they gained more assistance and more insight into the assignment by interacting directly with other students, yet they rated the vicarious sessions as being more "productive." Students, for the most part, felt comfortable participating in direct interaction sessions (Q4: SA = 10; A = 5). The literature has established that online computer conferencing, if successful, can establish a strong sense of social identity for its participants--see, for example, Gunawardena (1995) and Gunawardena and Zittle (1997). Thus, the student response here, if viewed in this context, is not surprising. If students feel connected to a group, the experiences within that group may be viewed more positively by its participants. Also, if given a choice, students would choose direct interaction (Q5: SA = 12; A = 3) over vicarious interaction (SA = 3; A = 5). This preference supports empirical evidence that students actually desire learner-learner interactions--see, for example, Grooms (2000).

Table 5: Students' Attitudes toward Vicarious and Direct Interaction Sessions

	SD	D	N	A	SA
1. I felt the sessions were productive ones.					
Vicarious	0	2	1	4	10
Direct Interaction	3	4	2	5	3
2. The sessions helped me to do the writing assignment.					
Vicarious	4	6	1	4	2
Direct Interaction	0	2	0	9	6
3. I felt I learned a lot about the topic from these sessions.					
Vicarious	3	5	1	4	4
Direct Interaction	0	2	1	7	7

4. I felt comfortable participating in the discussion.	na	na	na	na	na
Vicarious	0	6	2	5	10
Direct Interaction					
5. I would prefer this type of discussion forum in the future.					
Vicarious	2	6	1	5	3
Direct Interaction	0	0	1	3	12

Note: 5-point Likert-type scale: strongly disagree (SD), disagree (D), neutral (N), agree (A), strongly agree (SA). Numbers rounded to the nearest percentage.

Conclusions and Implications

Students' perceptions of their experiences during both types of sessions didn't necessarily coincide with their actual behavior during these sessions. Students clearly felt comfortable participating vicariously, yet, without direct interaction, reported that they didn't feel they learned as much and that these vicarious sessions didn't prepare them as well for the writing assignments as the interactive sessions did. When it came time to write the assignment after each discussion session, students wrote longer assignments and ones that referenced more topics of conversation from the group after vicarious sessions than they did after sessions with direct interaction. So even though students perceived that sessions with direct interaction were more useful to them in terms of the subsequent writing assignment, they actually produced more substantive written responses after vicarious sessions than they did after interacting directly.

Similarly, during these vicarious sessions, students actually did spend more time reading the contributions of other students than they had during direct interaction sessions. Also, during interactive sessions, students spent more time producing new topics of conversation than they did responding to the topics of other students. Perhaps because of this pattern of interaction (more topics than comments), students felt that they were garnering more useful bits of information, yet did not incorporate these ideas into the subsequent writing assignment to the same degree as they did after participating vicariously.

Although maybe not perceived as such by students, both vicarious and interactive sessions seemingly did engage them, albeit in different ways. Interactive sessions promoted more original discussion on the part of students while vicarious sessions, where students were separated from direct interaction, provided more time for students to read and reflect on the discussions of other students, and these ideas had more of a carryover to the subsequent writing assignment. Thus, a real pedagogical benefit was derived from vicarious interaction, although students didn't perceive it as such. One might argue that this type of interaction taking place when students weren't participants wasn't vicarious interaction, but a form of what Soo and Bonk (1998) describe as "learner-self" interaction, where the learner examines his viewpoint from another perspective, such as balancing different sides of an issue or reconciling one's opinion with the opinions of others. However, if that were the case here, we might expect to see more topic responses in writing assignments subsequent to vicarious sessions, rather than a heavier emphasis on comments, that is, synthesizing and summarizing (and, by extension, interacting with) the conversation of others.

What is significant to note here is that courses featuring interaction do not necessarily have to limit these experiences to direct interaction. As previously indicated in the literature (Sutton, 2001), this initial case study supports the notion that students may benefit from interacting vicariously. The social constructivist model assumes that students should be interacting with each other actively and directly for knowledge-making to occur. Rovai (2001) suggests that instructors should shape an online community that capitalizes on the medium's ability to support collaborative learning. Lapadat (2002) argues that constructivist online courses "are interactive and text-based." However, not every type of learner in every type of situation may benefit from direct interaction. We already understand that certain types of student personalities and learning styles (for example, students experiencing communication anxiety) may make certain students feel uncomfortable with direct interaction. Course designs that allow for opportunities for vicarious interaction may benefit not only these students, but other students in the course as well. For example, recognizing that some benefit may exist to vicarious interaction allows an instructor freedom to move beyond traditional synchronous and asynchronous conference-type communication in an online course. In fact, many new technologies in recent years (blogging, podcasting, simulations, etc.) don't readily support group interaction, whether it be synchronously or asynchronously, but still may provide useful and productive learning opportunities to students in the context of creating a community of learners.

References

American distance education consortium guiding principles for teaching and learning. (2005). Retrieved October 4, 2005, from http://www.adec.edu/admin/papers/distance-teaching_principles.html.

Anderson, T.D., and Garrison, D.R. (1995). Critical thinking in distance education: Developing critical communities in an audio teleconference context. *Higher Education*, 29, 183-199.

Best practices for electronically offered degrees and certificates. (2001). Western Cooperative for Educational Telecommunications. Retrieved December 5, 2005, from http://www.wcet.info/resources/accreditation/Accrediting%20-%20Best%20Practices.pdf

Bull, K. S., S. L. Kimball, and S. Stansberry. (1998). Developing interaction in computer-mediated learning. ERIC, ED 417902.

Fulford, C. P., and S. Zhang. (1993). Perceptions of interaction: The critical predictor in distance education. *American Journal of Distance Education,* 7(3), 8-21.

Grooms, L. (2000). *Interaction in the computer-mediated adult distance learning environment: Leadership development through on-line distance education.* Unpublished doctoral dissertation, Regent University, Virginia Beach.

Gunawardena, C.N. (1995). Social presence theory and implications for interaction and collaborative learning in computer conferences. *International Journal of Educational Telecommunications*, 1(2/3), 147-166.

Gunawardena, C.N. and Zittle, F.J. (1997). Social presence as a predictor of satisfaction within a computer-mediated conferencing environment. *The American Journal of Distance Education*, 11(3), 8-26.

Hewett, B. L., and C. Ehmann. (2004). Preparing educators for online writing instruction: Principles and processes. Urbana, IL: National Council of Teachers of English.

Herring, S. (1999). Interactional coherence in CMC.*Journal of Computer-Mediated Communication* 4 (4). Retrieved January 6, 2006, from http://www.ascusc.org/jcmc/vol4/issue4/herring.html .

Honeycutt, L. (2001). Comparing e-mail and synchronous conferencing in online peer response. Written Communication, 18(1), 26-60.

Irani, T. (1998). Communication potential, information richness and attitude: A study of computer mediated communication in the ALN classroom. *ALN Magazine*, 2(1). Retrieved December 1, 2005, from http://www.aln.org/alnweb/magazine/vol2_issue1/irani.htm.

Jakupcak, J., and M. S. Fishbaugh. (1998). A horse of a different color: Distance education; making it effective. ERIC, ED 417 894.

Jiang, M., & Ting, E. (2000). A study of factors influencing students' perceived learning in a web-based course envrionment. *International Journal of Educational Telecommunications*, 6(4), 317-338.

Jonassen, D., Davidson, A., Collins, M., Campbell, J., & Haag, B.B. (1995). Constructivism and computer-mediated communication in distance education. *The American Journal of Distance Education*, 9(2), 7-26.

Lapadat, J. C. (2002).Written interaction: A key component in online learning. *Journal of Computer-Mediated Communication,* 7 (4). Retrieved December 1, 2005, from http://www.ascusc.org/jcmc/vol7/issue4/lapadat.html .

Loban, W. (1976). *Language Development*, National Council Of Teachers of English: Urbana, Illinois.

Mabrito, M. (2006). A study of synchronous versus asynchronous collaboration in an online business writing class. *American Journal of Distance Education,* 20(2), 93-108.

Mabrito, M. (2004). Guidelines for establishing interactivity in online courses. *Innovate, 1*(2). Retrieved November 5, 2005, from http://www.innovateonline.info/index.php?view=article&id=12.

Moore, M. B. (1992). Distance education theory. *The American Journal of Distance Education,* 5(3), 1-6.

Northrup, P.T., (2002). Online learners' preferences for interaction. *Quarterly Review of Distance Education*, 3(2), 219-226.

Palloff, R.M., & K. Pratt. (1999). *Building learning communities in cyberspace.* San Francisco, CA: Jossey-Bass.

Rovai, A.P. (2001). Building classroom community at a distance: A case study. Education Technology Research and Development, 49(4). Retrieved August 12, 2005, from http://www.aect.org/pdf/etr&d/4904/4904-02.pdf.

Su, B., Bonk, C. J., Magjuka, R., Liu, X., & Lee. S. (2005). The importance of interaction in web-based education: A program-level case study of online MBA courses. *Journal of Interactive Learning*, 4(1). Retrieved February 6, 2006 from http://www.ncolr.org/jiol/issues/PDF/4.1.1.pdf

Soo, K., & Bonk, C.J. (1998). Interaction: What does it mean in online distance education? Paper presented at the ED/MEDIA/ED-TELECOM 98 World Conference on Educational Multimedia and Hypermedia & World Conference on Educational Telecommunications, Frieburg, Germany. (ERIC Document Reproduction Service No. ED 428724)

Sutton, L. (2001). The principle of vicarious interaction in computer-mediated communications. *International Journal of Educational Telecommunications,* 7(3), 223-242.

Swan, K. (2001). Virtual interactivity: Design factors affecting student satisfaction and perceived learning in asynchronous online courses. *Distance Education*, 22(2), 306-331.

Continuing the Dialogue

Research Blogging in Interior Design Graduate Education

Marlo Ransdell

Purpose

The purpose of this study was to examine interior design graduate student learning styles and the frequency of interaction within online weblogs centering on design research. Using asynchronous computer-mediated communication (CMC), students are able to interact with others engaged in a design research process regardless of geographic and time differences. Also, the focus on integrating research into interior design education has recently been added to accreditation standards set forth by the interior design accrediting body the Council for Interior Design Accreditation (CIDA). This study sought to uncover graduate student learning characteristics and their use of online discussions for further exploration of applications of online learning techniques in interior design educational and research.

Background

Previous research in online discussions show that cultivating online relationships, providing feedback, and reflecting on others' opinions can increase interactivity and scholarship among students resulting in a higher order of creative thought (Dutt-Doner & Powers, 2000). Reflective writing activities are also recognized as a way to enhance critical and creative thinking in students and have applications in all disciplines (Cisero, 2006). For interior design, research–based design relies on reflective writing to integrate existing literature findings into current design solutions. Using research in design education is also seen as a way to advance the scholarly culture of interior design and bridge the two diverse practice and academic worlds (Dohr, 2007). Interior Design graduate students engaged in a research agenda can benefit from online discussions and reflective writing supported by online discussions through networking, sharing ideas and resources, and reflecting upon divergent opinions within a group of peers.

This study also focuses on the specific learning styles of graduate students involved in online discussions about design research. The Myers Briggs Type Indicator (MBTI) has been used in determining typologies of students within different fields (Myers & McCaulley, 1985). It has also been used in interior design education and can help identify the characteristics of interior design students and their preferred learning styles (Russ & Weber, 1995). This study uses the MBTI to identify the learning styles of a group of graduate students. The MBTI is a series of 96 questions that yield a four-letter learning type. The 8 variables create a total of 16 learning types that emerge; E(extrovert) – I(introvert), S(sensing) - N(intuitive), T(thinking) – F(feeling), and J(judging) – P(perception). Each variable set is scored with one variable becoming dominant. Measures of attitude are seen in the first and last letters of the learning type. The middle two variables in the learning are ways that people gather and process information. This instrument has been used successfully in identifying learning styles of interior design students and distance education users (Portillo & Dohr, 1994; Russ & Weber, 1995; Mupinga, Nora, & Yaw, 2006). The MBTI types are further classified according to Keirsey and Bates (1974) to represent 4 distinct sub groups. These types are the Catalyst (NF) "writers who wish to inspire and persuade", the Traditionalist (SJ) "nurturing, conserving, and a historian", the Visionary (NT) "explore ideas and strive to find out the why of the universe", and the Troubleshooter (SP) "those who gravitate towards action (Russ & Weber, 1994, p. 33)". These contain characteristics that may determine the choices that people make in their work and school life (Keirsey & Bates, 1974).

Methodology

The sample for this study was 26 graduate students enrolled at Florida State University, a CIDA accredited school. The make up of the class was 23 females and 3 males. This module was used in conjunction with a graduate level Design Issues course that met face-to-face once a week. The online learning community Designscholar was designed with Moodle, an open-source course management software. It is free and available on the internet through moodle.org. This study module took place from September 3, 2007 – October 7, 2007. Permission was asked of all participants and appropriate human subjects forms were submitted and signed by all participants. The PI tracked and calculated survey data from the Myers-Briggs Type Indicator (MBTI) and tracked frequency of participation.

The first week of the module required students to post one introduction, the subsequent weeks asked each to post one time and respond one time. This resulted in a minimum number of 9 posts and responses, or interactions, for the duration of the 5-week module. The minimum amount of interactions was set so that interaction could truly be measured above and beyond a certain required amount. Setting a required amount was important for comparison of levels of involvement between groups. Attempts were made in the formulation of the module to increase participation and motivation to engage participants in discussions, such as using a personal web log that allowed for each individual's personality to be represented. Forced involvement many times leads to less quality and critical discourse, therefore the research relied on the personal motivation of students to engage and communicate.

Results and Conclusions

During this module there were 104 original article reviews posted by the 26 participants. The most referenced journals were Journal of Interior Design, Contract Magazine, Interiors and Sources, and Design Studies. About half of the articles posted came from refereed journals and were located initially through Informedesign.com. The other half came from popular press and various online websites.

The data from the MBTI has been collapsed following Keirsey and Bates (1974) four sub groups. This study further pairs these learning styles sub groups with the frequency of use of weekly online discussions. Information on learning styles of the sample and descriptive statistics of frequency of use are explored as predictors of use in online discussions.

Table 1: Type Distribution across Sample Groups

Sample	Catalyst (NF)		Visionary (NT)		Traditionalist (SJ)		Troubleshooter (SP)	
	n	%	n	%	n	%	n	%
Pilot Sample (n=26) *ID Masters Students*	18	69.2%	3	11.6%	5	19.2%	0	0.0%
*ID Study Sample** (n=234) *ID Masters Students*	94	40.2%	52	22.2%	58	24.8%	30	12.8%
*Normative Data*** (n=3008)	493	16.4%	310	10.3%	1394	46.3%	811	27.0%

* Data from: Russ, R. & Weber, M. (1995). Personality types of interior design students: Implication for education. *Journal of Interior Design*, 21(1), 30-38.

** Data from:Myers, I.B. (1962).*The Myers-Briggs Type Indicator*. Palo Alto, CA: Consulting Psychological Press.

National data on the MBTI reports that the percentage of the nation population that holds the N variable is 26.7%, this is the least frequently represented of the 8 variables (Myers, et.al., 1998). The pilot sample percentage was 80.8%, the most frequent variable. This resulted in 21 of the 26 participants being NF and NT sub groups, which are also the least represented sub groups in national data. The pilot study found that learning styles of these graduate students was consistent with other studies of learners in applied art fields (Portillo & Dohr, 1994; Russ & Weber, 1995). The preliminary findings of the pilot study confirmed previous research in the learning styles of design students where the N variable is represented significantly higher than the national population average. These findings suggest the sample was more alike in their learning styles than they were different.

Table 2: Frequency of Use across Student Group Types in Pilot Sample

Required Sample	Actual	Percentage over		
		# interactions	# interactions Difference	required# interactions
Pilot Sample n=26	234	396	+162	69.2%
Catalyst (NF) n=18	162	300	+138	85.2%
Visionary (NT) n=3	27	39	+12	44.4%
Traditionalist (SJ) n=5	45	57	+12	26.7%

The resulting number of interactions during the module was 396. The average number of interactions per person was 15.2, which was 6.2 interactions over the minimum required. This resulted in participation of 69.2% over the required minimum for the group. The sub group NF participated 85.2% more than required, while the SJ group participated 26.7% more than required. The NT group participated 44.4% above the minimum.

The overall findings suggest that interior design graduate students are more often intuitive learners in their school related tasks. The NF group was involved in the online discussions at a higher percentage rate than the other groups. This may be because N types are characterized as those who; make inferences about other's words and actions, read between the lines, prefer situations that allow speculation for future possibilities, and are unmotivated when forced to deal with facts and details (Quenk, 2006). Online discussions may offer intuitive learners an appropriate forum to explore their ideas and respond to the ideas of others. The sensing population, those who gather information through their five senses, used the online discussions slightly above the module requirements. They may see this as a tool for expression of ideas, but it may not be a natural fit, as it is with other learning styles.

This experience was seen as a success for all groups due to the class percentage of interactions that was received. Online discussions through research based blogs can produce thoughtful discussions leading to critical thought in research and adding to the growing body of knowledge in the interior design field. This research showed the response frequency rate for the 26 students in the study was 69.2% above the required number of online responses. During the pilot study, the online means of communication was seen an appropriate tool for the specific sample of interior design graduate students due to aspects of their learning styles being overwhelmingly similar.

References

Cisero, C. (2006). Does reflective journal writing improve course performance? *College Teaching*. 54, 2. 231-235.

Dohr, J. (2007). Continuing the dialogue: Interior design graduate inquiry and scholarly culture. *Journal of Interior Design*. 33(1), v-xvi.

Dutt-Doner, K.M. & Powers, S.M. (2000). The use of electronic communication to develop alternative avenues for classroom discussion. *Journal of Technology and Teacher Education*, 8(2), 153-172.

Keirsey, D. & Bates, M. (1974). *Please understand me*. Del Mar, CA: Prometheus Nemesis Book Company.

Mupinga, D., Nora, R., & Yaw, D. (2006). The learning styles, expectations, and needs of online students. *College Teaching*. 54, 1. 185-189.

Myers, I.B. (1962). *The Myers-Briggs Type Indicator*. Palo Alto, CA: Consulting Psychological Press.

Myers, I. B. & McCaulley, M. (1985). *Manual: A guide to the development and use of the Myers-Briggs Type Indicator*. (2nd ed.) Palo Alto, CA: Davies-Black.

Myers, S. A., Zhong, M., & Guan, S. (1998). Instructor immediacy in the Chinese college classroom. Communication Studies, 49, 240-253.

Portillo, M. & Dohr, J. (1994). *Bridging process and structure through criteria*. Design Studies. *115, 4. 403-416*.

Quenk, N. (2000). *Essentials of the Myers-Briggs Type Indicator assessment*. New York: Wiley.

Russ, R. & Weber, M. (1995). Personality types of interior design students: Implications for education. *Journal of Interior Design*. 21, 1. 30-38.

Developing Communities of Practice Amongst e-Learning Students

A New Zealand Story

Trevor Nesbit

The aim of this paper is to explore how concepts of Communities of Practice from the Knowledge Management literature can be applied to the interactions between groups of students studying in eLearning mode.

A literature review was conducted that explored the concept of a Community of Practice from the Knowledge Management literature, which then moved on to look at how these concepts could be applied in an eLearning context. Particular attention was paid to the work of Iverson and McPhee (2002), Wenger (1998), Polanyi (1996), Stenmark (2002), Nesbit (2004), Nonaka and Takeuchi (1995), Skryme (2001) and Harris and Niven (2002). The concepts of "knowledge of persons as subjects and knowledge of persons as objects" as described by Matheson (2008) are also explored as well as their linkages to students involved in eLearning courses.

Twelve eLearning practitioners in New Zealand from a variety of subjects were interviewed, with each interview focussing on their experiences of the emergence of a community of practice amongst their eLearning students.

The outcomes of the study included that a community of practice is more likely to emerge amongst a group of eLearning students when:

- The students have a passion to deepen their knowledge and interact with others about the topic.
- The students already know each other, or are given a chance to get to know each other in person as part of the course.
- The students are familiar with using the technology to socially interact.
- The students are from similar contexts and/or share similar experiences.

The results of the study are important as they highlight a number of concepts related to communities of practice from the knowledge management literature that provide a window of understanding for what takes place amongst groups of eLearning students, and as such would be of useful source of discussion for a variety of eLearning practitioners in a wide range of subject areas.

Introduction

Much has been written about the role that Communities of Practice (COP) play in Knowledge Sharing and Knowledge Management (KM). The purpose of this paper is to explore how the concept of a COP from literature within the KM field can be applied within an eLearning context.

A literature review will be summarised to help identify the main components of a COP from a KM perspective, particularly from a knowledge-sharing context. This review includes the work of Iverson and McPhee (2002), and Nonaka and Takuechi (1995) amongst others. These components, in particular those relating to knowledge sharing, are then applied to an eLearning environment, with some of this being based on the work of Harris and Niven (2002). The work of Matheson (2008) as it relates to alienation and the knowledge of persons (both as object and subjects) is briefly reviewed to create some additional context.

Results of interviews with a number of eLearning practitioners are presented and analysed with a view to exploring the applicability of the KM COP concepts in their experiences. The eLearning practitioners interviewed were all delivering courses within the tertiary education sector in New Zealand.

Methodology

The methodology used to complete this study was made up of three phases. The first phase was to conduct a literature review that explored the concepts of communities of practice in the Knowledge Management domain and their application into eLearning.

The second phase was to use the results of the literature review as a basis for conducting interviews with a range of eLearning practitioners in New Zealand and summarising each of these as a mini case study.

The final phase was to analyse the results of each interview to find linkages between the experiences of the eLearning practitioners and the literature on communities of practice from the Knowledge Management domain.

Literature Review

Communities of Practices within Knowledge Management

Iverson and McPhee (2002) describe two different approaches to knowledge management (KM).The information based approach, which is all about codifying and storing information and knowledge, and the people or interactional-based approach which is more about connecting 'knowers' (ie the people that know things) together.

Strongly connected to the people or interactional-based approaches to KM is the concept of a community of practice (COP). This concept is described by Wenger (1998) as a set of people who "share a concern, a set of problems, or a passion about a topic, who deepen their knowledge and expertise in this area by interacting on an ongoing basis". Wenger also describes how a COP has three elements: firstly "mutual engagement" by its members to enable knowledge to be shared; secondly a "shared repertoire", which is the resources for negotiating meaning including stories, jargons, theories and forms; and thirdly the "Negotiation of a Joint Enterprise", which gives a sense of coherence and purpose to the COP.

Another concept connected strongly to the people- or interactional-based approaches is that of tacit knowledge and in particular the differences between tacit knowledge and explicit knowledge. Polanyi (1966) as cited in Stenmark (2002) describes how the phrase 'tacit knowledge' refers to knowledge that cannot be easily articulated, and thus only exists in people's hands and minds, manifesting itself through actions; and goes on to describe 'explicit knowledge' as being knowledge that has been captured and codified into manuals, procedures and rules, and is easy to disseminate."

The differences between the information-based approach and the interactional- or people-based approaches (Iverson and McPhee, 2002) are similar in nature to the differences between information and knowledge as described in Nesbit (2004). In this study, which involves a summary of Iverson and McPhee (2002) and surveying the views of a number of KM practitioners, one of the most significant differences between information and knowledge involves the concept of context. Nesbit (2004) goes on to highlight the difficulty of creating technology based systems to store knowledge when the context of the person who needs the knowledge is unknown at the time the knowledge is stored.

Nonaka and Takeuchi (1995) as cited by Stenmark (2002) suggest that tacit knowledge becomes explicit through the process of externalization – that is the sharing of metaphors and analogies during social interactions.

This sharing of metaphors and analogies during social interactions enables the context of the person who needs the knowledge to be understood by the person who knows the knowledge.

Skryme (2001) identified two complimentary perspectives of knowledge management that emerge from the distinction between explicit and tacit knowledge. One of these is the nurturing of knowledge networking, where there is an emphasis on managing knowledge workers and the environment in which they work; in order to access the tacit knowledge is inside people's heads. This involves:

- Creating "communities of practice"
- Designing knowledge sharing workspaces
- Encouraging learning and innovation
- Practicing skilful dialogue and story-telling, with the aim of encouraging tacit knowledge development and sharing

Skryme (2001) goes on to describe how the nurturing of knowledge networking and the creation of communities of practice can enable the social interactions described by Nonaka and Takeuchi (1995).

Communities of Practice applied to eLearning

Harris and Niven (2002) describe a project where a collaborative online environment was developed that enabled communities of interest to meet and share experience and understanding of a particular subject. They go on to describe how this project related to communities of practice as described by other writers (Wenger, 1998). The main findings of this piece of work were:

- That the type of community that was required for this project was one that existed as "social relationships based on locality and neighbourliness, fellowship, a sharing of responsibilities, and a furtherance of mutual good through understanding and the exercise of natural sentiment", and that it would be useful to replicate this type of community in an online learning communities.
- The importance of social networks for online communities
- That an online community needs the added dimension of computer systems to support the social interaction of the members
- That the sense of shared purpose or ownership is difficult to develop within a distributed community.

Given that Nesbit (2004) highlighted some of the difficulties of using technology to share tacit knowledge from within a KM context; that Harris and Niven (2002) addressed the difficulty of developing a shared sense of purpose amongst the members of an online learning community; and that Nonaka and Takeuchi (1995) highlight the importance of social interaction for a community of practice, this suggests the following:

- That the best learning or sharing of tacit knowledge requires social interaction and that this needs to take place in a face-face setting. It is very hard to replicate this learning using technology
- That the shared sense of purpose needed in an online learning community is difficult to create when the members are distributed

It follows from this that two of the biggest challenges for the success of eLearning or an online learning community are to find ways in which tacit knowledge can be shared effectively amongst the members, and to find ways in which the members can develop a shared sense of purpose

The Implications for Successful eLearning

What does this all mean for the success of eLearning, particularly when the knowledge or learning that is being shared is at the tacit end of the explicit knowledge to tacit knowledge continuum? This continuum has parallels in Bloom's Taxonomy of Learning as described in Clark (1999). According to this, the lowest level of skills demonstrated by learners is typically the recall of data, whereas at higher levels the emphasis is on applying skills and knowledge to specific tasks (or contexts). Does this mean that the need for social interaction and a shared sense of purpose is not as important where the learning is at a lower level?

It may be that the learning needs of students at the lower end of Bloom's Taxonomy are such that social interaction and a shared sense of purpose are important, even though the knowledge that is being shared is at the more explicit end of the continuum. At the higher end of Bloom's Taxonomy, it may be that it is the tacit nature of the knowledge being shared that determines the need for social interaction and a shared sense of purposes, as oppose to the learning needs of the individual learner.

This suggests that the need for social interaction and a shared sense of purpose is present for learners at all levels of Bloom's Taxonomy, and that achieving this with technology is a significant challenge. It is worth considering techniques that can be used in an attempt to achieve this, with an eventual view to evaluating their relative successes.

Alienation and the Knowledge of Persons

Matheson (2008) describes the concept of alienation that comes about from the increasing use of electronic communication and how this relates to people having fewer close personal friends than they did twenty years previously, while being connected to many more people than they were by electronic means such as mobile phones, email and social networking websites such as Bebo.com and Facebook.com.

Matheson (2008) goes on to explore the concepts of "knowledge of persons as subjects" and "knowledge of persons as objects", with the distinction between the two being that when someone knows someone else as an object, then they know things about the person, which could include where they live and what sort of music they like. However, when someone knows someone else as a subject, they actually know the person. Matheson (2008) goes on to describe for the increased use of electronic communication is a driver for there being less communication that is personal than twenty years earlier because people are tending to know each other as objects rather than subjects.

In an eLearning context this would suggest that the students (unless there is some other contact between them) are likely to know each other as objects rather than subjects, and as a result have a lower level of communication that is personal. A consequence of this is likely to be that their level of interaction will not be as deep and therefore not as meaningful, and that the degree of social interaction may not be as high.

Being able to develop "knowledge of persons as subjects" amongst a group of eLearning students may therefore be a key to developing a COP amongst them as this would enable the development of social networks whose importance was highlighted by Harris and Niven (2002) and social interactions as described by Nonaka and Takeuchi (1995).

Interviews with eLearning Practitioners

Twelve eLearning practitioners in New Zealand were interviewed with a view to exploring how they address some of the issues that have been raised relating to COPs within an eLearning context. At the start of each interview a number of issues were discussed including:

- The level of study that their students were studying at.
- The extent to which the course had some face-face delivered components
- Whether the group of students were part of other courses that had face-face components
- Were the students studying an information technology related course

The results of the interviews are summarised in Table 1 which shows the concepts that are emerging from each one.

Table 1 : Concepts Emerging From Each Interview

Case	Concepts Emerging
1	• The importance of the students having mutual engagement, or choosing to enrol in the course in enabling communities of practice to emerge • The importance of social interaction between students engaged in eLearning courses in enabling communities of practice to emerge
2	• The importance of students being familiar with the use of the technology in the formation of a community of practice • The importance of students having passion for the topic in the formation of a community of practice
3	• The importance of students being familiar with the use of the technology in the formation of a community of practice • The importance of students having passion for the topic in the formation of a community of practice
4	• The importance of students having passion for the topic in the formation of a community of practice • The importance of the students having a desire to deepen their expertise in the formation of a community of practice
5	• The importance of the students having mutual engagement, or choosing to enrol in the course in enabling communities of practice to emerge
6	• The importance of face-to-face contact between the students in the emergence of a community of practice • The importance of the students having shared experiences in enabling a community of practice to emerge
7	• The importance of social interaction between students engaged in eLearning courses in enabling communities of practice to emerge • The importance of students being familiar with the use of the technology in the formation of a community of practice
8	• The importance of social interaction between students engaged in eLearning courses in enabling communities of practice to emerge • The importance of students being familiar with the use of the technology in the formation of a community of practice
9	• The importance of social interaction between students engaged in eLearning courses in enabling communities of practice to emerge • The importance of the students having shared experiences in enabling a community of practice to emerge
10	• The importance of social interaction between students engaged in eLearning courses in enabling communities of practice to emerge • The importance of students being familiar with the use of the technology in the formation of a community of practice

11	• The importance of students being familiar with the use of the technology in the formation of a community of practice • The importance of the students having a desire to deepen their expertise in the formation of a community of practice
12	• The importance of social interaction between students engaged in eLearning courses in enabling communities of practice to emerge • The importance of students having passion for the topic in the formation of a community of practice

Case Number 1

This eLearning practitioner described the experiences of working with two different groups of students in different contexts, with neither group studying courses that were related to information technology.

The first group of students were studying a fully online course that is part of a full time programme of study where the predominant delivery is face-face mode. The students were enrolled in the final year of a three year of an under graduate degree. Because of the regulations surrounding the course at the time it was not possible to make participation in online discussion forums compulsory.

There was a varied level of participation in the online discussion forums, however the students that chose to participate more benefited from interacting with others, and as the students knew each other from their other courses, the COP amongst them developed reasonably quickly. One of the significant factors in a number of the students choosing to not interact via the online discussion forum appeared to be that they had not chosen to do this course online as it was a compulsory requirement of their programme of study.

The second group of students were a group of post graduate students who were studying a fully online course where they were not part of a face-face delivered course at all. The emergence of a COP amongst the students was hindered slightly by the students not having met face-face, with this being confirmed by an increase in online interaction after a face-face workshop part way through the course. An aspect that helped with the emergence of the COP with this group was that the students had chosen to enrol in this course as part of their ongoing professional development.

The experiences with both of these groups point to the importance of the concept of "mutual engagement" as described by Wenger (1998), and the important of social interaction as described by Harris and Niven (2002).

Case Number 2

The students involved were studying a course a part of their on the job training for a particular trade, with the level of study being lower than the first year of an undergraduate degree. The course was delivered fully online with the students not having any face-face contact from other courses. The content was not information technology related.

The students were required to answer questions on an online web based discussion forum, with a very low level of participation resulting indicating that a COP not really formed amongst the group of students. A significant contributing factor was that with the students having no face-face contact with each other, it made it more difficult for a COP to emerge. This is consistent with the importance of social interaction as described by Harris and Niven (2002). In addition to this, the group of students were preparing for a trade, and not really "wanting to study" and therefore not having as much motivation to "share a concern, a set of problems, or a passion about a topic" as per Wenger (1998).

Another factor that hindered the emergence of a COP amongst this group of students was a perceived lack of literacy and/or familiarity with the technology being used. This was partially borne out when the students were able to participate in the discussion using text messaging via their mobile phones. This change related in a significantly higher level of participation. This was partly due to these students being comfortable using text messaging to socially interact, whereas they were not as comfortable using web based online discussion forums for social interaction. This is also consistent with the importance of social interaction described by Harris and Niven (2002).

Case Number 3

The students were studying a graduate diploma, where the entire qualification is delivered fully online, with the content being information technology related to an extent. When this qualification was created, it was created as a fully online qualification, with its ongoing success being the successful formation of a COP amongst the students within each course. Some of the success factors in the creation of the COPs within the groups of students included:

- That the creation of an environment that allows for the emergence of a COP needs to be an intentional move, and that it should not be left to chance.
- That the students "share passion about a topic" and desire to "deepen their expertise by interacting on an ongoing basis", both of which are consistent with the ideas of a COP described by Wenger (1998)
- That because of the content being related to information technology, the students had a degree of familiarity with the technology

Case Number 4

The students were a group of people from the same profession who chose to enrol in a fully online course as part of their professional development. The content was not related to information technology. A very successful COP appeared to emerge amongst the students, with the critical success factor being that the students chose to be involved in the course so that they could deepen their knowledge about the topic. This is very similar to the ideas of "sharing passion about a topic" and having a desire to "deepen their expertise by interacting on an ongoing basis" as per Wenger (1998).

Case Number 5

The students were studying a course as part of the second year of a three year undergraduate degree where the content is not related to information technology, although the students do have a reasonable degree if literacy with information technology. The course was a traditional face-face delivered course with all material for the course available online. The students were encouraged to participate in optional online discussion forums.

A COP appeared to form for those who chose to participate, and the knowledge shared appeared to enhance their learning. This is consistent with the idea of mutual engagement and having a desire to interact on an ongoing basis (Wenger, 1998). The issue being contemplated at the time of this interview was about how to make participation in the online discussion forums compulsory for all students, while retaining the benefit of the COP that comes from mutual engagement

Case Number 6

Two groups of students were studying a fully online qualification at a level just below degree level, with the qualification being completed part-time over the course of a year. One group of students were employed in a specific role in a specific industry, with the other group being from a variety of roles in the public sector. The content included generic knowledge and skills that can be used across a number of industries and was not related to information technology. Both groups of students had some face-face contact during workshops that took place part way though each of the courses that made up the qualification.

In the first group (with specific roles in the same industry), a COP emerged quite quickly. The main reason for this was seen as being that the students had a shared concern and set of problems (Wenger, 1998) from being in the same roles in the same industry.

In the second group, it took longer for the COP to emerge. The reasons for this were seen as being:

- That there was a culture within the public sector that did not encourage the sharing of knowledge and experience. This highlights the importance of developing a culture that facilitates the sharing of knowledge and is consistent with the importance of finding ways to encourage tacit knowledge sharing as described by Skryme (2001).

- The experiences of the students had to be made more abstract for commonalties to become apparent, thereby enabling shared concerns and problems to become apparent. This is consistent with the concept of context (Iverson and McPhee, 2002)

In both groups, the workshops that took place part way through the course enhanced the COP, although that was not the original intent of the workshops. The original intention of the workshops was to clarify requirements of the course; however the most valuable aspect, particularly with the second group, was to enable social interaction (Nonaka and Takeuchi, 1995) between the students. In both groups of students, the degree of interaction between the students increased after the workshops had taken place, suggesting that the social interaction that took place did enhance the COP.

Case Number 7

Two groups of students were studying a course at first year degree level, with one group of students being predominantly part time and studying in online mode, with the second group studying the course in traditional face to face mode as part of a full time programme of study. The content of the course is significantly information technology related.

Both groups of students were required to participate in an online discussion forum, with each group being in a separate discussion forum. The COP emerged quite quickly amongst the second group of students, but took significantly longer with the first group. The main factor for the difference appeared to be the social interaction that already existed between the full time face to face students enabled them to interact in a more meaningful manner, whereas this was not the case with the students that were only studying online. This is consistent with the importance of social interaction described by Harris and Niven (2002).

In a subsequent semester, both groups of students were put into the same online discussion forum. The students that were studying in online mode only appeared to have a higher degree of interaction earlier than if they had been in their separate online discussion forum. This could be pointing to the idea that it is easier to join a COP that has already emerged successfully, particularly if there is already a degree of social interaction present.

Case Number 8

The students were studying a group of three courses that are part of the final year of a three year undergraduate degree programme and can be studied by students enrolling in other degree level qualifications at the same institution. These particular courses are delivered online, whereas all of the other courses in this degree are delivered in face to face mode. The content of all three of the courses are to an extent related to information technology, with the entire degree being related to information technology. At the start of each of the courses as one hour introductory face to face tutorial is held where the students are able to meet each other so that they can gain some degree of familiarity with how else is enrolled in the course as well as learn about how the course is organised.

The COP emerges reasonably quickly amongst the students who are studying towards the information technology related degree as these students already know each other and already have a degree of social interaction as per Harris and Niven (2002), and are more than competent users of the technology. However, the students studying these courses towards other qualifications, many of who have English as a second language, do not participate to the same extent. As a direct result of this subsequent offerings of this course are going to include some optional face to face tutorials that will create an opportunity for social interaction amongst these students, thereby creating more opportunities for them to participate in the COP that emerges.

Case Number 9

The students were studying an online delivered second year degree level course that is part of a full time qualification that is strongly information technology related. Most of the other courses that the students are studying are delivered in face to face mode which means that most of the students already know each other. A small number of students were part time students who were working full time in information technology related fields. The content of the course is related to "soft skills" as opposed to technical skills.

The COP emerged quite quickly amongst all of the students, both full time and part time, due to two main factors. The full time students already knew each other and already had a degree of social interaction outside of this course with this being consistent with the social interaction concepts described by Harris and Niven (2002). With the part time students who were working in information technology related fields, they had experiences that were in common and as such had a degree of shared sense of purpose and shared sets of problems as described in Wenger (1998).

Case Number 10

A diploma that is the equivalent to the first year of an undergraduate degree was developed for online delivering to technicians in widely dispersed and isolated rural communities, with the development of the diploma having been described in McCarthy and Ross (2005). The purpose of the diploma was to provide information technology skills to a person in each of a number of rural communities so that they could provide information technology support to the local school and other organisations within their communities. The students were brought together 2-3 times each year during the diploma for face to face block courses.

A number of issues emerged with the formation of a COP amongst the group of students who were enrolled. The one of most significance appeared to be that the students did not have a desire to have a high degree of social interaction. This was borne out to an extent with some of the students choosing to live in isolated communities because they did not want to have a high degree of social interaction. That a COP had difficulty in forming amongst the students is consistent with the ideas of the desire to "interact on an ongoing basis" as described by Wenger (1998) and the importance of social interaction described by Nonaka and Takeuchi (1995), Skryme (2001) and Harris and Niven (2002).

While the students involved in this diploma were familiar with the technology being used (as it was the content that they were studying), they did not typically use the technology for social interaction. In the words of the eLearning practitioner interviewed "they were more likely to socially interact with a fishing rod than with PC".

The face to face block courses that were held did aid the emergence of a COP to an extent, which is again consistent with the ideas regarding social interaction expressed by Nonaka and Takeuchi (1995), Skryme (2001) and Harris and Niven (2002).

Case Number 11

The students were studying a first year degree level information technology related course that was being delivered in online mode to a group of students as part of a business related diploma. A small group of students enrolled in the first offering of the online version of the course as pilot. Half of the students only enrolled in the online version of the course because of timetabling problems, with another subset of the students knowing each other from outside of studying.

A number of issues arose with the emergence of a COP amongst this group of students including:

- With some of the students enrolling in the online version because of a timetabling problem, they did not have the desire to be interacting online on an ongoing basis, which is consistent with the desire to "deepen their expertise by interacting on an ongoing basis" as described by Wenger (1998).
- Some of the students who knew each other from outside studying chose to interact outside of the online platform, which in effect created a separate COP which a number of the students could not participate in, and as a result did not benefit from the interactions that were taking place.

Case Number 12

A number of information technology related courses were delivered via online and video conference mode to secondary school students in remote rural secondary schools. Many of the students enrolling had a strong desire to be studying the particular content and had no other way of studying it. The academic staff member involved in delivering the courses visited each school at least once during the year.

The COP appeared to emerge quite quickly amongst the students as they had a real desire to study the content that was on offer which is consistent with the ideas of Wenger (1998) about "sharing a passion for the topic". The visits from the academic staff member to each school also server to enhance the COP, and the use of video conferencing appeared to enhance the COP as it appeared to provide for more social interaction, as per Nonaka and Takeuchi (1995), Skryme (2001) and Harris and Niven (2002), than just the use of an online web based discussion forum.

Analysis and Discussion

In analysing the twelve cases that have been presented, a number of themes or concepts emerge that are consistent with the literature. These themes include that:

- It can be easier for a community of practice to emerge amongst a group of eLearning students when they have chosen to enrol in the particular course, and in particular have chosen to enrol in a version of the course that is delivered in online mode. This concept of mutual engagement in a community of practice is very similar to that described by Wenger (1998). That the students have chosen to enrol in the course at all suggests that they have a passion for the topic, and may be wanting to share their knowledge with others, with this concept being very similar to the idea of members of a community of practice being a set of people who "share a concern, a set of problems, or a passion about a topic, who deepen their expertise by interacting on an ongoing basis" (Wenger, 1998)
- If the students enrolled in a course being delivered online have either previously been enrolled, or are concurrently enrolled in other course, then a community of practice is likely to emerge faster as the students already know each other and have had some form of social interaction. This is consistent with the need for social interaction described by Nonaka and Takeuchi (1995), Skryme (2001) and Harris and Niven (2002).
- Familiarity with the technology is an important factor in students interacting in an online environment, and in particular, familiarity with using the technology to socially interact is an important factor in students

participating in online discussions. This is also consistent with the ideas of social interaction described by Nonaka and Takeuchi (1995), Skryme (2001) and Harris and Niven (2002).

- Students having shared experiences are more likely to form a community of practice as they have a shared sense of purpose which is similar to the "negotiation of a joint enterprise to give a sense of coherence and purpose" that is described in Wenger (1998). It is also very similar with the importance of context as described in Iverson and McPhee (2002).

The work of Matheson (2008) relating to alienation and the knowledge of persons creates an interesting window through which to view the interaction of students in an eLearning context, and in particular as to whether they do form a community of practice. There appears to be a link between the extent to which having the knowledge of persons as subjects (as opposed to objects) and the extent of meaningful interaction and sharing of knowledge between the people involved.

This becomes apparent in looking at a number of the cases explored whether the only contact between the students involved was online as opposed to being in person. In these cases the community of practice took longer to emerge and develop than where there was some contact. This became more apparent in the cases where there were some face-to-face interactions part way through a course, as in these cases the face-to-face contact helped to an extent with the formation of a community of practice, which could be due to the students being given the opportunity to develop some knowledge of each other as subjects as opposed to objects.

While this concept of the knowledge of persons as subjects and the knowledge of persons as objects was not a subject of the interviews that took place, it would appear that it does provide another context through which some greater understanding of the nature of communities of practice amongst groups of eLearning students could be gained. As such it provides an area in which further research could be conducted.

Conclusions

The aim of this study was to explore how communities of practices concepts from the knowledge management domain could be applied to an eLearning context through a review of literature and conducting interviews with a range of eLearning practitioners.

The main conclusions that can be drawn from this study are that:

- Students having passion to deepen their knowledge and interact with others about the topic are more likely to form a community of practice.
- Students who already know each other, or who are given a chance to get to know each other in person, are more likely to form a community of practice.

- Familiarity with the technology, and more importantly, familiarity with using the technology to socially interact is an important factor in the formation of a community of practice.
- Students from similar contexts and with similar or share experiences are more likely to form a community of practice.

Based on these conclusions, it can also be concluded that the concepts of communities of practice from the knowledge management domain do provide a window through which more understanding of an eLearning context can be gained, and that further exploration of how the knowledge of persons as subjects apply to students in an eLearning context would provide more opportunities for understanding.

The importance of these findings is that they provide a window through which more understanding can be gained of the interactions that take place amongst groups of eLearning students, and as such will be a useful source of discussion for eLearning practitioners wishing to provide better experiences for their students.

References

Clark, D. (1999). *Learning Domains or Bloom's Taxonomy*. Downloaded from http://www.nwlink.com/-donclark/hrd/bloom.html 1 March 2005.

Harris, R.A. and Niven, J. (2002) *Retrofitting Theory to Practice* – A Reflection on the Development of an e-Learning Community. Downloaded from http://www.scrolla.ac.uk 21 July 2005.

Iverson, J.O. and McPhee, R.D. (2002) *Knowledge Management in Communities of Practice*: Being True to the Communicative Character of Knowledge Management Communication Quarterly 2002.

Matheson, D. (2008) *Alienation and the Knowledge of Persons in the Networked Society*. Conference Presentation, Fourth International Conference on Technology, Knowledge and Society, Boston, January 2008.

McCarthy, C. and Ross, J. (2005) *E-Learning Initiative for Education in ICT*. Proceedings of the 18th Annual Conference of the National Advisory Committee on Computing Qualifications, Tauranga, July 2005.

Nesbit T. (2004), *Knowledge: More Than Information* – The Implications for KM Systems. Conference Presentation, Fourth International Conference on Knowledge, Culture and Change in Organisations, London, August 2004.

Nonaka, I. and Takeuchi, H. (1995) *The Knowledge-Creating Company*: How Japanese Companies Create The Dynamics of Innovation. Oxford University Press.

Polanyi, M. (1996) *The Tacit Dimension*, Routkedge and Kegan Paul (1998) in Knowledge in Organisation (ed L. Prusack), Butterworth-Heinemann.

Skryme D.J. (2001) *Capitalizing on Knowledge* – From eBusiness to kBusiness. Oxford: Butterworth-Heinemann.

Stenmark, D. (2002). *Sharing Tacit Knowledge*: A Case Study at Volvo, included in Barnes, S. (2002) Knowledge Management Systems: Theory and Practice. London: Thompson Learning.

Wenger, E. (1998). *Communities of Practice*. Learning, Meaning and Identity. Cambridge: Cambridge University Press.

Part III

Online Collaborative Learning

Making the Case for Mobile Collaborative Learning for Reading Comprehension on Handheld Computers

Jason Black and Lois W. Hawkes

Introduction

It is apparent that many problems plague American primary school students in the development of effective learning strategies. The decline in test scores and increased dropout rate show that educators and researchers are not meeting many of the educational needs of our students [Soloway & Norris, 1999; Norris, 1994]. Many students are showing apathy towards the learning process and are not interested in the material being presented or the methodology used to present that material. Researchers are perplexed about what is behind this trend, and how it can be halted.

The growth in population and economics in America has created two problems for educators. First, schools are experiencing an increase in diversity which leads to a complex learning environment. Secondly, technological advances are moving to schools, creating expectations that schools graduate literate and corporately competent students [Damarin, 1998]. This implies that students not only are able to read and write effectively, but also have literacy and expertise in the available technology.

Recently, efforts have been made to incorporate technology into the classroom to effectively enhance student learning and performance. Many of these advancements make use of constructivist theories, which assert that knowledge is not only transmitted from teacher to student, but is also built, or "constructed", in the mind of the learner [Lerner, 1997]. These systems allow students to take control of their learning, with the teacher as facilitator of the learning process.

One of the most successful constructivist learning techniques is collaborative learning, where students acquire and build their knowledge by interacting with others. Studies have shown that students often learn better in this type of environment than in the traditional classroom setting, since the success of each depends upon group success [Norris, 1994]. Here, students can share strengths with others in ways that would be difficult in the traditional competitive classroom. Current technology lends itself well to applying the collaborative approach to a variety of domains, but has not significantly been used outside of math and science.

Reading comprehension has emerged as an area requiring considerable attention in America, as schools throughout the county are facing a student population struggling to acquire this skill [Vaughn, Klingner & Bryant, 2001]. According to national studies, almost forty percent of fourth graders fail to read at grade level [National Center of Educational Statistics, 2005; Mathes, et. al, 1999], and this group has shown little change from 1992 until 2005. One reason for this deficiency lies in the diversity of school populations and teaching styles, where schools are more diverse than at any other time in the history of America [Mathes, Grek, et. al, 1999]. Developing an approach that is appropriate for all students is often difficult. Consequently, if left unattended, poor reading skills often leads to poor self-esteem, lack of discipline and a higher dropout rate [Juel, 1996].

According to the National Assessment of Education Progress [National Center for Educational Statistics, 2005]:

- Average reading scores for fourth graders showed thirty-six percent (36) reading below grade level, twenty-five (25) percent reading at grade level, thirty-one (31) percent reading proficiently and eight (8) percent reading at advanced level; this shows little change from 1992 to present
- Students at higher percentiles made gains between 1992 to 2000, while students at the lower percentile lost ground

An additional study by the National Center for Learning Disabilities [Lyon, 1999] illuminated the following:

- Reading failure has reachede epidemic proportions in the United States
- Children who do not learn to read constitute seventeen percent of the total population and over fifty percent of the special education population

So it is clear that reading comprehension is a serious problem impacting our society.

Many non-technological strategies have been developed to deal with this problem. Several of these programs have shown significant improvement in reading comprehension skills. Among them are Peer-Assisted Learning Systems (PALS), Reciprocal Tutoring, and Question-Answer Relationships

(QAR). While each has been successful in given scenarios, the latter, QAR, has been a particularly effective supplement to a classroom reading program. QAR teaches students to read by recognizing relationships between questions and sources of information, either in the text or in the reader's experience [Raphael, 1982]. Despite successful strides made with QAR, the effectiveness of combining this strategy with successful computer-based learning techniques – and, more specifically in a mobile environment - has yet to be examined. Thus, this work proposes a mobile learning environment that uses QAR as a framework in an effort to present an effective collaborative reading comprehension tool. The tool is designed for implementation on a personal digital assistant (PDA) to take advantage of the mobility of today's users, and incorporates strategies that can serve as a template for mobile collaborative learning systems. It is proposed that the combination of gains seen from QAR and mobile collaboration can make a significant contribution to the crisis in reading comprehension.

Related Research

Class-Wide Peer Tutoring (CWPT)

Class-Wide Peer Tutoring (CWPT) was developed by researchers [Delquadri, Greenwood, Stretton & Hall, 1983] as a method for improving overall student achievement and academic response time. In CWPT, students serve in reciprocal roles – each serving as both tutor and tutee during an academic session. Students can receive one-on-one peer sessions, immediate critiquing from classmates, and social and academic inclusion during the same session. Some of the benefits of CWPT instruction methods include a) more time on task, b) immediate feedback through peer error-correction, c) practice in both teaching and learning, and d) more social and academic inclusion from peers [King-Sears & Bradley, 1995].

CWPT has proven successful in a variety of disciplines. Many of the advancements have been in math and spelling, but other areas shown gains as well, such as word definitions, identifying examples and non-examples of concepts, procedural steps for problem solving, mapping skills and cause and effect situations [King-Sears & Bradley, 1995]. While there have been several successes in the use of CWPT [Greenwood et. al, 2001; Fuchs et. al, 2001], there has been little research in how effective the application of technology would be in this effort. Further, much of the CWPT research has been limited to basic facts and computation problems [Fuchs et. al, 1995]. It would be valuable to investigate applying CWPT to more cognitive aspects of learning, such as reading comprehension.

Peer-Assisted Learning Strategies (PALS)

Several extensions of the CWPT theory have been developed and implemented successfully, among these Peer-Assisted Learning Strategies

(PALS), developed by Fuchs and colleagues [Fuchs, et. al., 2001; Fuchs, Fuchs & Kazdan, 1999]. In PALS, higher-level readers are paired with lower-level readers in reading activities, such as story sharing, sounding out words or other phonological sounds, and paragraph summarization. These students alternate roles during these activities, thus gaining experience as both teacher and student. In these studies, the students have consistently shown greater progress than their counterparts in non-PALS classrooms.

It is clear that PALS has been proven to be an effective tool for improving reading skill acquisition and reading comprehension across various reading levels and grades. What is not known is how effective such a strategy could be when coupled with the computer technology currently available. A merging of this type of collaborative technique with the real-time communication facilities of a computerized environment can only serve to enhance the gains already seen by such a strategy such as PALS.

Reciprocal Teaching / Tutoring (RT)

Reciprocal Teaching (RT), developed by Palincsar and Brown [Palinscar & Brown, 1984], is an instructional approach where teachers and students share in the role of leading discussions through dialogue. The purpose of the dialogue is to bring about full understanding of material read through the application of four comprehension strategies: prediction, questioning, clarification and summarization [Palincsar, 1991]. The strength of RT is that it concentrates on forming skills that teach students how to read to learn as opposed to learning to read. The overall goal of RT is to enhance the comprehension skills of readers who have not benefited from traditional instructional methods through collaborative dialogue. This communication serves to build skills useful for extracting meaning from reading texts [Palincsar & Klenk, 1992].

In all, RT has been proven to be a successful method of cognitive strategy instruction with all grade levels and across student distinctions. Yet, there are many issues to yet be explored involving the application of RT to the current technologically enhanced classroom, as not much work has been done to date on examining the effect of merging this methodology with a computerized learning environment.

Question-Answer Relationships (QAR)

The Question-Answer Relationship (QAR) strategy was developed by Taffy Raphael [Raphael, 1982] as an instructional activity for helping students develop reading comprehension skills by answering questions based on text. In defining this paradigm, Raphael developed four question types that dictate the processing of information in the text. These question classifications include "Right There" questions (the answer is located within the text in an easily located sentence), "Think and Search" questions (the answer is located in the text within two or more sentences), "Author and You" questions (the answer is located in the text but is not stated explicitly), and "On Your Own" questions (the answer is not located in the text but requires input from the user's prior background knowledge). This classification of questions has been shown to be an effective method of teaching students how to answer questions independently.

QAR has been beneficial to educational research in that it not only has demonstrated the ability to improve comprehension skills of student participants, but has also shown effective implementation of peer-assisted learning strategies. It is not clear to date whether applying QAR to a computerized learning environment would produce a more efficient reader. That area is one rich is potential and worthy of investigation.

Mobile Learning (M-Learning) in Collaborative Learning Environments

Technological advances are creating an environment where people are working while in motion, or across vast distances, both in the corporate and educational settings. And the classroom in particular is a ripe location for advances in mobile learning (m-learning), which occurs when users collaborative via wireless communication using handheld computers or devices – cell phones, personal digital assistants (PDAs), pagers, etc.). To be more specific, learning is occurring in a mobile context with the aid of handhelds [Attewell, 2005]. Current research shows that schools are finding handhelds to be particularly attractive for use in classroom learning, due to the smaller cost, portability, durability and increasing advancements in wireless technology [Soloway & Norris, 1999]. And, researchers are investigating more strategies to incorporate the technology seamlessly in the curriculum and make it obtainable to children from diverse backgrounds [MIT Media Lab, 2006].

The technological services available in mobile environments lend themselves well for collaboration – chat features, instant messaging, email, etc. – which can serve to create a very robust and effective learning environment [Isaacs, Walendowski & Ranganathan 2002]. Consequently, it is prudent to examine methods to incorporate mobile collaboration in the standard classroom learning activities. Researchers are now seeing the potential of this endeavor, and are beginning to scratch the surface of the enhancement to learning that is possible when employing these techniques. This work is a proposal of one such approach.

Using Speech in Mobile Learning Environments

It is important that researchers be able to facilitate mobile users' interactions as best as possible, by providing a variety of modalities for communication [Nanavati, Rajput, Rudnicky, & Siconni, 2006]. Virtually all mobile devices have capability for speech input, usually in the form of *distributed speech* [Schmandt, Lee, Kim & Ackerman, 2004]. In this environment, speech is captured on the mobile device, and sent across a wireless network to a server, where processing is done. The translated text is then returned to the device for use. There are several issues to examine here, such as speech quality, network bandwidth and latency, background noise, etc. This work, however, will present an interface mechanism for facilitating voice input in a mobile collaborative learning session; the examination of the aforementioned issues are being examined and will be presented as future work.

System Design Issues

High-Level System Description

The system modeled in this research was centered on reading comprehension, attempting to combine the benefits of a proven collaborative learning strategy with the innovation of technology. The process model of this system is the Question-Answer Relationship (QAR) collaborative reading strategy mentioned earlier. In a given session, the user begins a session by entering his id, which is checked for validation. If a match is found, information for that user is downloaded to the PDA, which includes the icon used to represent that user and the series of lessons, questions, and question type problems. The user then indicates that he or she is ready to begin, as illustrated in Figure 1.

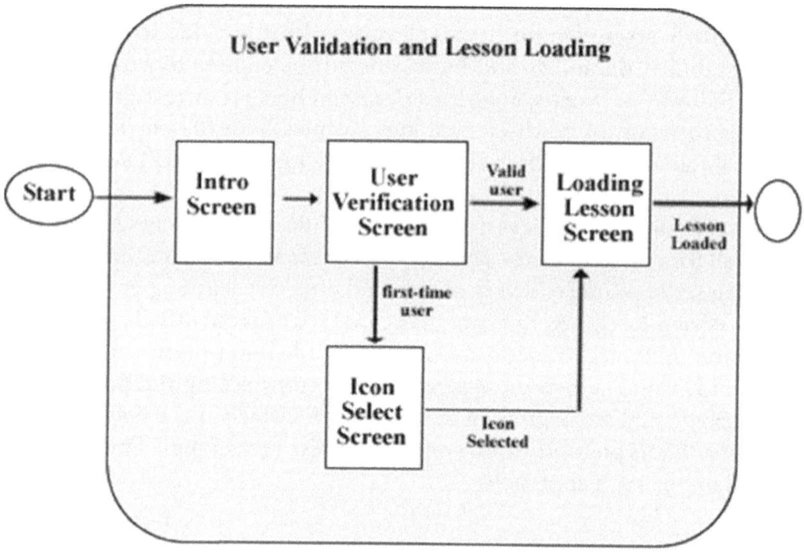

Figure 1: Process Flow Diagram: User Validation Phase

The system then presents the user with first the lesson screens (in this case, story pages to be read), and upon completion of reading a series of questions is presented. After these questions have been answered, they are checked for correctness. If there are any incorrect answers, the user is returned to the question answering phase, and is now allowed to collaborate with his or her partner (using shared workspace, chat, email, etc.) to reach a consensus on these answers. If all of the questions are correct, the user then is quizzed on the type of question that was asked (using Raphael's taxonomy of questions), and again, consensus must be reached if any are answered incorrectly. This process is illustrated in Figure 2.

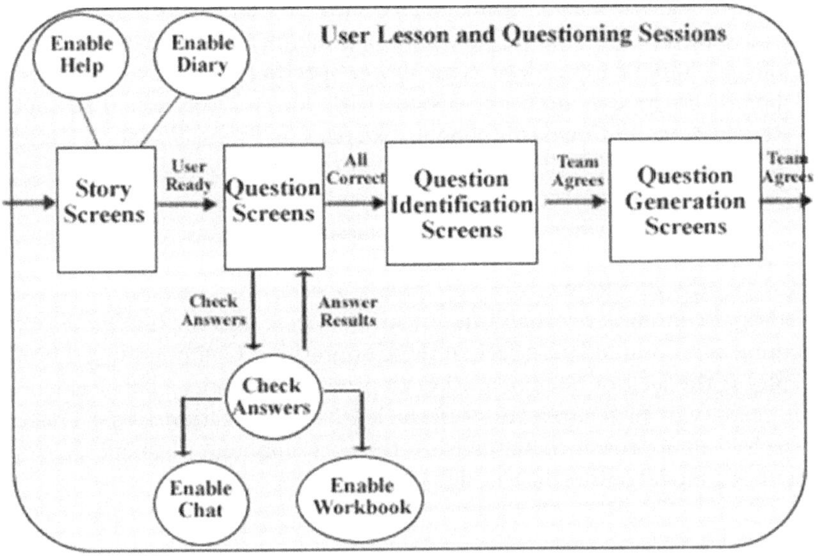

Figure 2: Process Flow Diagram: User Lesson and Questioning Phases

Once the process is completed, users are asked (reciprocally) to generate questions of category types defined in QAR. These questions types are randomly selected by the system, and a record of user answers is maintained. Upon completion of a session new material is downloaded from the server and the process repeats until the user wishes to quit. Again, all input is captured using the mechanisms available on all PDAs – using keypad entry via stylus, transcription of written text, and speech or audio input.

Challenges to Development of the Interface

The design of an interface to achieve this model is in a mobile environment is subject to a number of constraints compared to desktop applications [Paelke, Reinmann & Rosenbach, 2003]. These include:

- Limited screen resolution: Typical resolutions on mobile devices range from 100*80 pixels for mobile phones to 240*320 for PDAs (compared to mega-pixel displays in desktop environments).
- Small display dimensions: The size of the device greatly impacts the sophistication and robustness of any interface, a problem that is not so evident on desktop platforms.

- Limited number of colors: Many mobile devices that have color displays are yet limited to several thousand colors (compared to desktops capable of millions of colors).
- Limited processing power: Mobile devices are severely restricted in this area, which controls the level of animation, video and complex graphics presented.
- No standardization of input mechanisms: While desktop applications can typically rely on the presence of a number of standardized input devices, mobile input devices are device specific. Many have no full keyboard, no mouse, pointing devices with lower resolution (i.e., touch screens), or additional components like pens on PDAs. Phone and pagers have no pointing devices at all.
- Auditory environment: Developers must be cognizant of use of sound in a public setting, where noise can be an issue.

In short, the development of any mobile application, particularly one including the innovative capabilities mentioned here, has the burden of overcoming or accommodating each of these limitations. Compounding this difficulty is the lack of documentation to provide assistance. This has led to the scarcity of such applications in the learning application arena. This research is an approach to standardize these components through development of a model of interface design strategies.

System Implementation

Development and Testing of Proposed Design

In order to arrive at an optimal interface design, the researchers conducted a Paper Prototype Test to determine if the planned design was feasible and practical [Black, Hawkes, Jean-Pierre, Johnson & Lee, 2004]. The study was done using elementary students ranging from second to fourth grade with varying reading levels and technology backgrounds. The test was conducted using Snyder's recommendations regarding number of participants (five students were used), length of test (thirty minute segments), and number of tasks (five basic system tasks) [Snyder, 2003]. The results showed that this design was indeed practical – students were able to manipulate interface features easily and effectively; students preferred speech over other forms of input; and students indicated no difficulty in reading text on the small screen or in progressing through the required tasks. It was the results of this study that lead to the structure of the final system.

Resulting System Architecture

The system architecture resulting from the paper prototype test is designed on the infrastructure approach for wireless communication [SEIR-TEC, 2002], where mobile devices are served by a central access point and communicate with this point via the network, as illustrated by Figure 3. This is consistent with the configuration of most handheld devices, which generally communicate with a host network to obtain applications in order to minimize device power consumption. In this system, the handhelds download the application and user-specific data (progression data, user interface layout preferences, etc.) at the start of a session, and "synch" with the server, uploading user specific information back to the server for storage in the database.

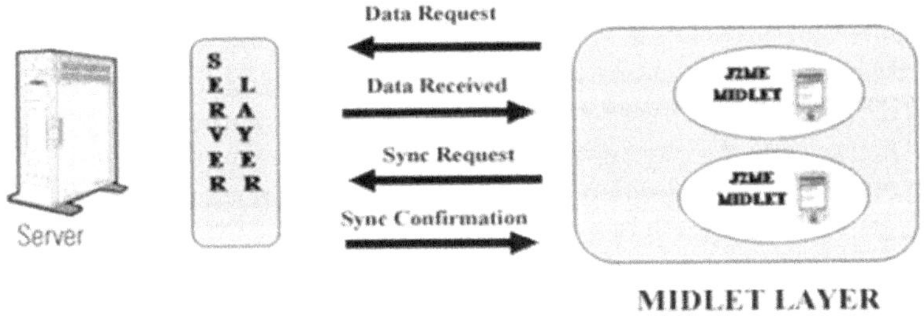

Figure 3: Layout of System Architecture

The server handles the following activities:

- Managing login and security issues
- Monitoring student progress through sessions
- Downloading interface status to handhelds
- Translating speech to text on receipt of audio input
- Monitoring security / functionality of shared workspaces during learning sessions
- Receiving student progression data from handhelds at the completion of a session
- Generating student progression reports at end of each session
- Monitoring IM requests to instructor from students

Each handheld device manages the following tasks:

- Presenting the system interface according to student preferences
- Monitoring student progress through the learning sessions
- Monitoring student tendencies while working with the interface
- Facilitating the utilization of shared workspaces during collaboration
- Providing chat services via written and/or voice input
- Packaging up and distribute audio input to the server for processing
- Allowing for adjustment of the interface features (colors, menus, etc.)
- Submitting student progress and tendency data to the server at end of the session
- Allowing for students to submit instant messages (IMs) to instructor or partner

Description of Interface Components

The interface design centers on a teamwork-oriented learning environment, with students working in pairs to collaborate on understanding domain-specific lesson material (in the present case, reading comprehension). The interface is interactive, with students communicating in real-time through the provision of a chat feature. The system also contains a database that keeps track of student pairs and their progress through instructional sessions, tracking team accuracy and performance. The learning application presents domain-specific lesson material in increasing difficulty and complexity in successive sessions, helping to building the knowledge base of the student participants.

The user interface system contains the following components:

1. Several*login screens*, where user input can be given via text or audio as illustrated in Figure 4 below:

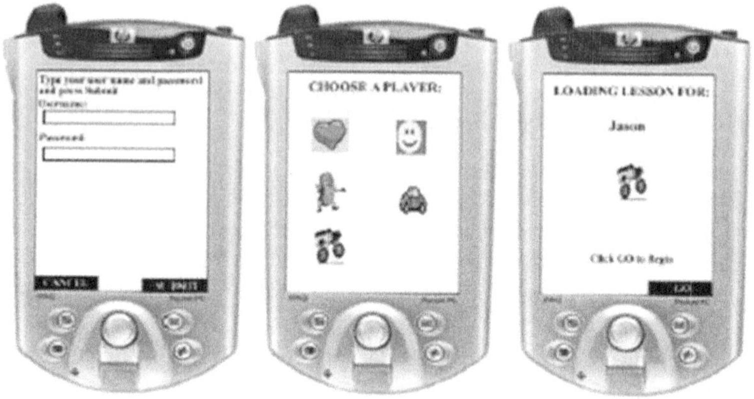

Figure 4: Series of Login Screens

2. A *Shared Lesson Feature,* containing the working material for each session, visible by both partners. This area contains the story or questions to be completed, and a session status area containing current score and icons showing the avatar of the user's partner, as illustrated in Figure 5 below.

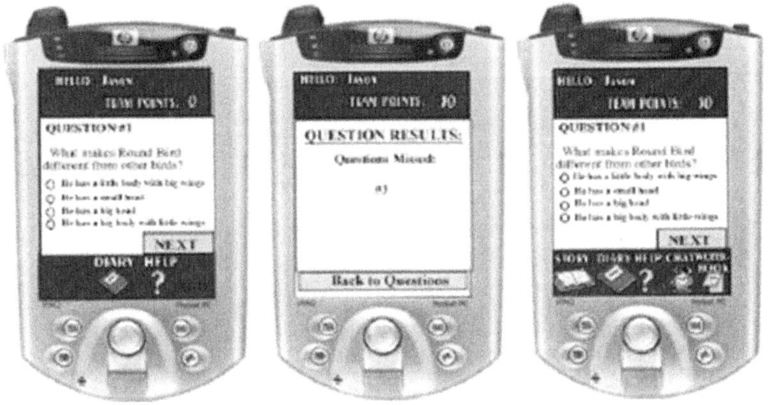

Figure 5: Question Screens with Icons below

The first screenshot shows the system when collaboration is off – only the personal journal (the Diary) and the Help icons (the question mark) are active. Once the user answers questions, if any are missed, the collaborative features (the Group Workbook (which is shared), and the Chat Feature) are turned on, and the team may collaborate on the answering of these questions.

3. The *Collaborative Features*, which are used by partners to have dialogue, resolve conflicts, and reach consensus. This consists of a group notebook, which contains logged information about accuracy and tendencies during learning sessions for periodic student reflection, and chat screens, which allow students to communicate with each other instantly. This is shown in Figure 6 below.

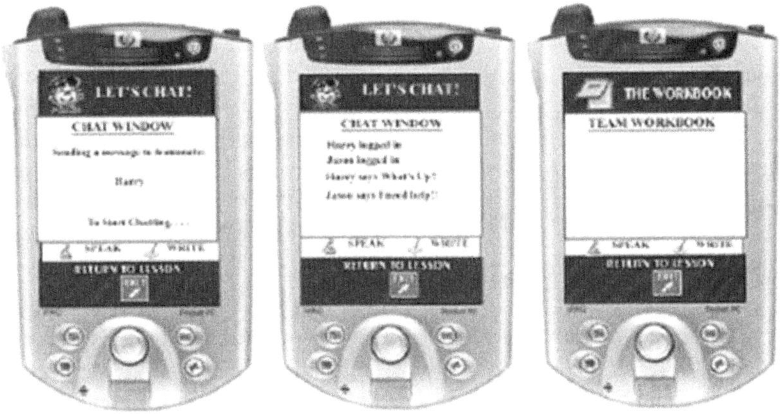

Figure 6: Chat screens and Group Workbook

4. A *Personal Reflection and Assistance Feature*, where students can log personal comments or feedback about their learning session; and a *Get Help Feature*, which is used to send messages to the instructor when assistance is needed, as shown in Figure 7.

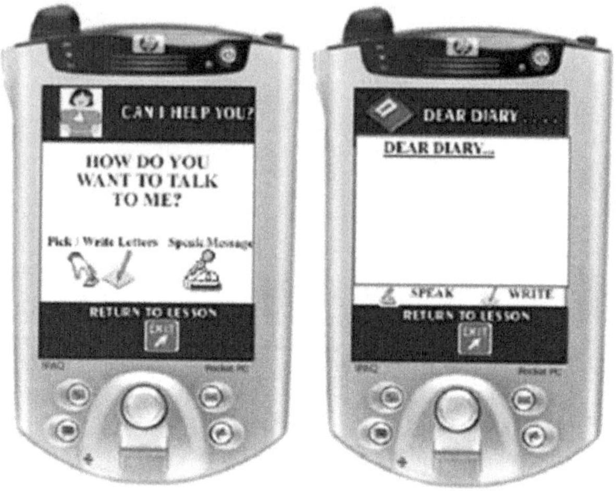

Figure 7: Get Help and Personal Diary Screens

These interface features are designed to present the key components that collaborative software should exhibit [Churchill & Snowden, 1998] – shared context, awareness of others, and negotiation through communication. It is the belief of the researcher that these design strategies employed in a collaborative handheld wireless environment will serve to significantly improve the learning ability of student participants exposed to the system.

Implementing Standard Input

Textual input is captured using the standing mobile device techniques available on most devices - pen or stylus via keypad entry, and both the Letter Recognizer and Transcriber (written text using the stylus). The handling of the input and format in which this is done is device specific, and beyond the scope of this research. These screens also include the standard menu layout available on most mobile devices, appearing at the bottom of the display just above soft buttons. Users select these menus by clicking on them and choosing the appropriate function.

Additional Input – Speech Recognition

As illustrated earlier, the accommodation of younger users is a very important design feature, as it may often be difficult for an elementary-level student to have the coordination or dexterity to handle the stylus or transcriber. As a result, this system is designed to facilitate *Speech Input*, where users can speak their input via the standard microphone available on mobile devices. This input is then captured by the application, and packaged and sent to the server, where it is then (via Java Servlet) converted to text (illustrated in Figure 8). The converted text is then returned to the device where it is displayed on the screen (or sent via email if needed).

It is important to note that, to date, there are no reading comprehension systems using voice input and collaboration on the handheld platform. The input problem is not evident in math and science domains, where input is simply selecting items or entering numbers into equations. In a more complex learning interaction that is presented in reading comprehension, the problem is much more difficult to address. Speech or voice input fills this void perfectly and provides a simple yet effective alternative.

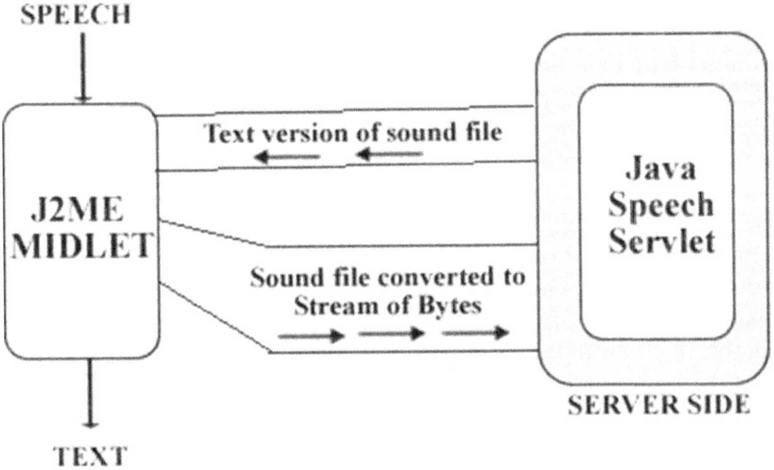

Figure 8: Diagram of Prototype Processing of Speech Input

Conclusion and Future Work

This research illustrates that the development and implementation of this type of collaborative mobile learning application is indeed possible. The screens were implemented in Java (Java 2 MicroEdition, the Java suite designed specifically for mobiles), and MIDlets (J2ME's version of a Java Applet) were used to handle system functionality. The communication between devices and server was accomplished via wireless network and illustrates that such a system can indeed be employed in any wireless environment.

Designing the system with QAR as the central methodology was also accomplished. QAR requires individuals to work in pairs, and this interface facilitates this well. QAR also requires student pairs to read, answer questions and generate questions, and then identify categories in which questions belong. The screens developed in this system are designed with that goal in mind, and aid this process well. And, since QAR is a successful paper-base learning methodology, it is clear that this interface only enhances this process.

Speech input is also facilitated very effectively in this application. Students are able to speak verbally to partners, and see what they said in text on the screen. This is a very significant issue, for it removes the previous obstacle (particularly for younger users) of having to learn how to manipulate the stylus. It is easy to imagine how difficult having to use the stylus, keypad or transcribe large volumes of text could be for any user, particularly younger users. This interface removes that burden.

There are yet many areas of future work to be considered. For instance, the immediate next step is to implement this system in an actual reading classroom, with the intention of integrating this system into their learning curriculum as a successful tool. It is hypothesized that students exposed to this tool will improve reading comprehension ability, and the integration process will not be obtrusive to the learning process. Since most current reading comprehension software is developed for the desktop environment, utilization of such a system in this mobile platform could prove very exciting and rewarding, serving to fill a much needed void in the collaborative learning spectrum.

Overall, the system presented in this work is one attempt to introducing a collaborative mobile learning environment that is not math and science domain-specific, and that can serve as a template for mobile collaborative learning in general. This research is just scratching the surface of what is possible, and the future looks extremely promising for what can be done to turn this tide toward better readers nationally.

References

Black, J., Hawkes, L., Jean-Pierre, K., Johnson, I. & Lee, M. (2004). A Paper Prototype Study of the Interface for a Children's Collaborative Handheld Learning Application. In Proceedings of Mobile HCI 2004, Glasgow, Scotland. September 13-16, 2004.

Churchill, E.F. & Snowdon, D. (1998). Collaborative virtual environments: An introductory review of issues and systems. Virtual Reality: Research, Development and Applications, 3, 3 – 15.

Damarin, S.K. (1998). Technology and multicultural education: The question of convergence. Theory Into Practice, 37(1), 11 – 19.

Delquadri, J.C., Greenwood, C.R. Streeto, K. & Hall, R.V. (1983). The peer-tutoring spelling game: A classroom procedure for increasing opportunity to respond and spelling performance. Education and Treatment of Children, 6, 225 – 239.

Fuchs, D., Fuchs, L.S. & Kazdan, S. (1999). Effects of peer-assisted learning strategies on high school students with serious reading problems. Remedial and Special Education, 20(5), 309 – 318.

Fuchs, D., Fuchs, L.S., Thompson, A., Svenson, E., Yen, L., Al Otaiba, S., Yang, N., McMaster, K.N., Prentice, K., Kazdan, S. & Saenz, L. (2001). Peer-assisted learning strategies in reading: Extensions for kindergarten, first grade and high school. Remedial and Special Education, 22(1), 15 – 21.

Greenwood, C.R., Hou, L.S., Delquadri, J., Terry, B. & Arreaga-Mayer, C. (2001). The Classwide peer tutoring program: Implementation factors that moderate students' achievement. Journal of Applied Behavior Analysis, 25, 101 – 116.

Isaacs, E., Walendowski, A. and Ranganathan, D. (2002). Mobile instant messaging through Hubbub. Communications of the ACM, 45 (9). 68—72

Juel, C. (1996). What makes literacy tutoring effective? Reading Research Quarterly, 31, 268 – 289.

King-Sears, M.E. & Bradley, D.F. (1995). Class-wide peer tutoring: Heterogeneous instruction in general education classrooms. Preventing School Failure, 40(1), 29 – 35.

Lerner, M. (1997). The Current State of Technology and Education: How Computers are used in K-12 and Brown University Classrooms. http://www.netspace.org/-mrl/handbook/int_ed.html.

Mathes, P.G., Grek, M.L., Howard, J.K., Babyak, A.E. & Allen, S.H. (1999). Peer-assisted learning strategies for first-grade readers: A tool for preventing early reading failure. Learning Disabilities Research & Practice, 14(1), 50 – 60.

MIT (2006). MIT Media Laboratory. http:// www.media.mit.edu/about/ overview.pdf . (Summer 2006).

Nanavati, A., Rajput, N., A.I. Rudnicky, R. Sicconi (2006). Workshops: SiMPE: speech in mobile and pervasive environments. In Proceedings of Mobile HCI 2006, Helsinki, Finland, September, 2006.

National Center of Educational Statistics. (2005). National Assessment of Education Progress (NAEP) 2004 reading report card for the nation and states. Washington, D.C.: Author.

Norris, C.A. (1994). Computing and the classroom: Teaching the at-risk student. The Computing Teacher, 21(5), 12- 14.

Paelke, V., Reimann, C., & Rosenbach, W., (2003): A Visualization Design Repository for Mobile Devices. Proceedings of The Second International Conference on Computer Graphics, Virtual Reality, Visualisation and Interaction in Africa, February 3-5, 2003, Cape Town, South Africa.

Palincsar, A.S., & Brown, A.L. (1984). The reciprocal teaching of comprehension-fostering and comprehension monitoring activities. Cognition and Instruction, 1, 117- 175.

Palincsar, A.S. (1991). Reciprocal Teaching. http://www.ncrel.org/sdrs/ areas/issues/students/atrisk/at6lk38.htm.

Palincsar, A.S. & Klenk, L. (1992). Fostering literacy learning in supportive contexts. Journal of Learning Disabilities, 25(4), 211 – 225.

Raphael, T. (1982). Question-answering strategies for children. The Reading Teacher, 36, 186 – 190.

Schmandt, C, Lee, K, H, Kim, J, Ackerman, M. (2004). Impromptu: Managing Networked Audio Applications for Mobile Users. In Proceedings of MobiSys 2004, Boston, Massachusetts, June 2004.

Snyder, C. (2003). Paper prototyping: The fast and easy way to design and refine user interfaces. San Francisco, CA: Morgan Kaufman.

Soloway, E. & Norris, C.A. (1999). Schools don't want technology, schools want curriculum. http://www.cisp.org/imp/june_99/06_99-soloway-insight.htm.

SouthEast Initiatives Regional Technology in Education Consortium (SEIR-TEC) News-Wire, "Using Handheld Technologies in Schools" (2002), Vol. 5 (2).

Orsmond, P., Merry, S,. Reiling, K. (1996). *The Importance of Marking Criteria in the Use of Peer Assessment in* Assessment & Evaluation in Higher Education, **21**[3], 239-250.

Orsmond, P., Merry, S,. Reiling, K. (1997). *A study in Self Assessment: Tutor and Students' perceptions of performance* in Assessment & Evaluation in Higher Education, **22** [4], pp 357-369.

Orsmond, P., S. Merry and K. Reiling (2000). "The Use of Student Derived Marking Criteria in Peer and Self-Assessment." *Assessment and Evaluation in Higher Education* 25 (1): 23-38.

Orsmond, P., Merry, S. & Reiling, K. (2002) The use of formative feedback when using student derived marking criteria in peer and self assessment, Assessment & Evaluation in Higher Education, 27(4), pp.309-323.

Vaughn, S., Klingner, J. K., & Bryant, D. P. (2001). Collaborative strategic reading as a means to enhance peer-mediated instruction for reading comprehension and content area learning, Remedial and Special Education, 22 (2), 66 – 74.

Interactive and Collaborative Learning in an e-Learning Environment

Using the Peer Review Process to Teach Writing and Research Skills to Postgraduate Students

Arianne Rourke and Kathryn Coleman

Many educators have expressed the importance of providing feedback to students in higher education (Brown & Knight, 1994; Hounsell, 2003) and that formative feedback is recognized as important during the revision phase of writing (Flower, 1985; Topping, 1998). There have been many studies on the usefulness of peer review in higher education particularly for facilitating online learning (Carlson & Berry, 2003; Raadt, Toleman, & Watson, 2005). There has however, been contradictory evidence as to the reliability and validity of peer assessment (Brown, Bull & Pendlebury, 1997; Topping et al., 2000; Segers & Dochy, 2001) as it has been suggested that good students under rate their performance and less accomplished students often over rate their performance (Dochy Seger & Sluijsmans, 1999; Lejk & Wyvill, 2000). Students can misinterpret the assessment criteria (Orsmond et. al. 1996; 1997; 2000; 2002), causing confusion when comparing peer to teacher feedback. There has been a lot of focus in the literature on the process of peer review particularly as a tool for providing feedback. There has however, been less emphasis placed on the collaborative nature of the process and its value towards life-long learning. As Collins, Harkin and Nind (2001) explained "good learning is collaborative both because of the centrality of communication for learning and because thinking is, itself, a social practice" (p.110).

When peer review is used in an online collaborative learning (OCL) environment, as Brunk-Chavez and Miller (2006) discussed, collaborative learning can empower the student and "encourages exploratory talk" (p.5), which is above and beyond its role as an assessment tool. Rowland (2000) sees this interchange as a form of "collaborative enquiry" where "mutual support" (p.122) is provided. This paper will explore this concept within the framework of discussing the adoption of online peer review to teach Postgraduate students how to write a research paper in Arts Administration.

Introduction

The 21st century student in higher education is expected to be self directed and independent particularly as face-to-face teaching hours have been decreased in many degree programs. This has been balanced by an increase in the use of the world wide web, which has created an online information revolution that has had both a positive as well as a negative effect on education. As a result of this phenomenon, educators have needed to become more reliant on this technology to promote learning outside of the face-to-face classroom and as a tool for assessment within the course. Online learning and teaching has grown considerably in the last decade to include more flexible delivery modes, which works beyond the online 'drop box' for course material by facilitating the sharing of resources and promotion of asynchronous discussion. Within this eLearning environment students are expected to be active learners as they work towards timelines and common goals within a discourse community of learners. Within this learning environment the online student is expected to take initiative, be knowledgeable about using the technology and be willing to participate in online discussions and peer review often without much support. This virtual classroom if effectively utilised and well designed can facilitate and engage learning while creating a sense of community and promote collaboration between students and co-operation between teacher and student. Guglielmo (2005/6) suggested that "creating intentional and significant interactions among students through collaborative activity and group work becomes essential to connect students to the course" (p.104).

In the online learning space peer review has become a prevalent assessment tool for teaching and learning writing and research skills. The purpose of this paper is to discuss the importance of promoting collaboration in the eLearning environment in higher education focusing specifically on its role towards facilitating online peer review with Postgraduate students as a teaching method for assisting students towards writing a research paper on arts administration. In this discussion there will be an emphasis on the underlining generic skills that students can obtain from participating in the peer review process that can go beyond the initial goal of assessment and classroom learning towards the aim of acquiring life skills for their future profession as arts administrators. This paper examines the role that online collaborative learning (OCL) and peer review plays towards promoting the long-term retention of the learning of writing and research skills for Postgraduate students in the e-learning environment and seeks to contribute to the research in calibrated peer review (CPR™) and computer mediated peer review (CMPR) learning and teaching and post-graduate collaboration in research. These issues will be disseminated via two case studies, which showcase two approaches to using peer review to teach coursework Masters students how to write a 10,000 word research paper in arts administration. The first case study uses the anonymous and randomly allocated online CPR™(http://cpr.molsci.ucla.edu) system developed by UCLA, the second attempts to simulate the same system using online collaborative CMPR within the discussion forum and assignment tools in my eLearning Vista UNSW. This paper presents the triumphs and pitfalls of both systems within the theoretical framework of the higher education literature on teaching and learning and online peer review.

Online collaborative learning (OCL) in higher education

Learning to learn as well as learning to learn online have become key factors in the pedagogical frameworks in the teaching of disciplinary writing and research at College of Fine Arts (COFA), University of New South Wales (UNSW) in the Master of Art Administration (coursework). OCL has evolved in the last decade as the learning management system (LMS) has changed to address the necessity of the shortened teaching semester and cost effectiveness in the teaching and assessing of coursework masters degrees. Time deprived instructors seeking to develop pedagogically rich and effective learning experiences have in recent times seen the value of utilising LMS which do not place undue stress on the also time deprived Postgraduate student. An important aspect of this online environment is to provide well-planned OCL that supports the formation of an evolving learning community of practice (Levinsen, 2006; Bullen, 1998). Cecez-Kecmanovic and Webb (2000) forecasted that future eLearning environments should place importance on improving the outcome of OCL, with emphasis being placed on the design of these eLearning environments as well as the establishment of clear roles for both the instructor and the student within the virtual learning platform (Powers & Guan, 2000). Emphasis has also been placed on the importance of support and effective coordination of the collaborative learning process within the eLearning environment (Weinberger, Ertl, Fischer & Mandl, 2005). Dillenbourg (2002) also emphasized that blending collaborative learning with instructional design does have some pitfalls, however a balance of these with close instructor monitoring to guide the student through the learning process could be advantageous particularly when teaching research and writing skills that this paper addresses.

There have been many studies on the usefulness of peer review in higher education particularly for facilitating OCL (Carlson & Berry, 2003; Raadt, Toleman, & Watson, 2005). Including Brunk-Chavez and Miller (2006) that has suggested that collaborative learning can empower the student and "encourages exploratory talk" (p.5) between students as they explore their learning and conduct their research. As Postgraduate learners in a coursework degree a sense of community and interchange of ideas in the field is imperative. Peer review however, had its own issues particularly when implementing a student centred approach towards teaching research. The Research paper course aimed at directing the learners through a scaffolded approach where students learn both research methods and writing skills with the end goal of producing a chaptered research paper. The philosophy behind the Research paper, a core course in the Master of Art Administration recognises the importance of peer review, particularly for future art administrators who of necessity will be working in a collaborative context in the arts. Students research a topic related to the broad area of their Internship completed towards the end of their Masters degree with an arts industry placement that enables students to gain practical and supervised experience in the field of art administration including: gallery management in the public, private, commercial and not-for-profit sectors, curatorial practice, education and public programming and art writing. The online environment offers anonymity as directed by the instructor to allow students to learn by 'trial and error' while working at one's own pace through the assessment as well as providing a sense of 'think before you speak' not often available in the spontaneity of the face-to-face classroom and this aspect was crucial to students who worked or would in the future work as colleagues in the field. The value of having time to contemplate an answer leads not only to a sense of confidence in the writing process for the less accomplished student but also encourages the more confident student to be aware and to 'self review' their work as they are directed through the writing process together. This in turn is enhanced by the further input of the students' peers through the peer review process and collaborative learning in the online community.

Collaborative online peer review has played an important role in the Postgraduate coursework courses particularly in assisting with the writing process of chaptered research papers that demand a higher level of research and writing skills not previously required in other coursework subjects. Littleton & Hakkinen (1999) acknowledged learning together is a constructive process where "understanding...is mediated by and built up through interaction with others and meanings are negotiated and established through interaction in a wide range of social contexts" (p.24). Through the learning and teaching of this course the writers have found that peer review and collaboration for Postgraduate students is a valid mechanism for the evaluation of student's skills and abilities. This valuable learning experience for students is listed as an important UNSW graduate attribute where 'the skills required for collaborative and multidisciplinary work' and the 'capacity for analytical and critical thinking' alongside 'creative problem solving, are listed'. (UNSW graduate attributes). As previously mentioned, Collins, Harkins and Nind (2001) emphasised that "good learning is collaborative both because of the centrality of communication for learning and because thinking is, itself, a social practice" (p.110). This type of OCL and constructive criticism if conducted appropriately following a set criteria, can assist towards boosting a writer's confidence, provide a 'sense of community' for the student as they research independently and add peers points of view into a process that could be particularly isolating for many Postgraduate students (Mulder & Pearce, 2007). Rowland (2000) saw this interchange as a form of "collaborative enquiry" where "mutual support" (p.122) was provided. In this community of learner's students within the course management system WebCT Vista or through systems such as CPR™ make use of peer learning and collaboration as a learning tool. With this OCL peer review process involving both self-reflection and review, works along side peer-to-peer reflection, evaluation and review.

Peer review as a collaborative learning process

The Research paper course utilises self and peer assessment in thirty percent of the formative assessment which comprises of three stages where students write and review their own and other's proposal, contents page and literature review, while the remaining seventy percent is the submission of the research paper for assessment after a supervisor provides feedback via email of the draft paper. Many educators have expressed the importance of providing feedback to students in higher education (Boud, 1990; Brown & Knight, 1994; Biggs, 1999; Hounsell, 2003) and that formative feedback is recognized as important during the revision phase of writing (Flower, 1985; Topping, 1998). As student learning has become more motivated by feedback, peer review, peer mentoring and peer evaluation have enabled students to play an active role in the learning and assessment processes. Bower and Richards (2006) recognized how relevant collaborative learning can be "as opposed to direct instruction, collaboration allows students to actively participate in problem solving processes by communicating about the conceptual representations relating to the task at hand" (p.79). There has however, been contradictory evidence as to the reliability and validity of peer assessment (Brown, Bull & Pendlebury, 1997; Topping *et al.*, 2000; Segers & Dochy, 2001) as it has been suggested that good students under rate their performance and less accomplished students often over rate their performance (Dochy *et. al.*, 1999; Lejk & Wyvill, 2000). Students could misinterpret the assessment criteria (Orsmond *et. al.* 1996; 1997; 2000; 2002), causing confusion when comparing peer to teacher feedback as previously mentioned. Lindblom-ylanne, Pihlajamaki & Kotkas (2006) discussed that: "self and peer assessment are more than students grading their own or a peer's work, because the assessments involve students in determining what high-quality learning is in a specific case" (p.52). Determining this factor involves student's comparing their own work with their peers and Brookfield (2006) suggested that this critical reflection is especially important in the online environment. More research into the new assessment for learning shift has to be considered as the move from the more traditional testing strategies continues.

As with other studies in self and peer review (Lindblom-ylanne, Pihlajamaki & Kotkas, 2006, Cho & Schunn, 2007) issues amongst students included fears of plagiarism, peers evaluating too critically, the 'extra' workload and the structure of the learning and teaching within CMPR or in CPR™ are similar. An example of student discussion in the forum about fairness included "Does anyone else seem to think that if someone did not put much 'effort' into their review of your work, that it ultimately affects YOUR mark? I know I spent a great deal of time and effort trying to assist another student by giving useful feedback and suggestions, which I feel were not reciprocated - although perhaps this was not a bad thing as it meant they thought it was sufficient enough!" (Student feedback in the stage 1 discussion forum semester 2 2008). Depending on the cohort the level of discussion and cooperation in the LMS were noticeably different and therefore impacted on the peer review process and collaboration outside of the assessment process. As students self-direct and self govern their work, these Postgraduate coursework students have a good grounding in the discipline having already completed at least eight courses within the degree so they can add valuable insights and critical skills into the OCL peer review process and collaborate further as learners and mentors in the research process. The twelve-week intensive Research paper course is a fully online research core where students are also given both oral and written instructions at meetings when required particularly at the beginning of semester. Guglielmo (2005/6) discussed how "instructors require their online students to attend at least one class meeting at the beginning of the course in order to provide a basic introduction to course assignments and expectations" (p.106). Cooper (1999) as Guglielmo (2005/6) later suggested, identified that this meeting in the learning process is a needed and essential part of OCL. The writers have found that the online collaborative learning process has worked best when interactions both online and face-to-face have occurred across the semester. Optional face-to-face meetings have been initiated to address issues as the students' individual and group issues have arisen. These issues have differed with each cohort of students, so flexibility on the part of the instructor is a vital factor towards keeping the lines of communication 'alive and well', which is an important underlining objective of all successful OCL models.

Case study one: Using CPR to collaboratively teach how to write a research paper in a coursework masters degree

CPR™ was first utilised in 2007 when the Research paper course went fully online. The Research paper course as previously mentioned, had thirty percent of the assessment peer reviewed and graded online using CPR™. As part of the course assessment, students were required to review other student's work through CPR™, an example of an online web-based peer review and assessment system that is learner centred. It was initially used to manage the review process in the Research paper course because it allows students to collaborate as researchers and as students through the submission of assessments, peer review work and self review in a computer mediated system. The instructor sets the submission dates and the CPR™ program provides average marks for each assessment task (Rourke, Mendelssohn, Coleman, 2008). This structured online procedure taught students how to write to criteria through a scaffolded approach through worked examples of poor, average and good writing to teach and assist the learner with the assessment for learning process. CPR™ randomly sorts and anonymously distributes papers to students and calibrates the grades. It uses a four-step process of:

Task→Calibration→Peer review→Self-assessment.

Problems such as students discomfort, defensiveness and time limitations were important factors that the instructor considered when deciding whether to try a different OCL peer review system a year later. Peer review in the discussion forum or as CMPR has now been used for one year with differing results. As previously mentioned, the CPR™ process for the students involved reviewing good, average, and poor examples of each assignment. In the CPR™ process students are scored on their calibration, and they are not allowed to proceed until the calibration tasks have been passed. In this system students submit their text to CPR™, before the time for text submission elapsed. When the text entry time was over, students logged into the CPR™ system again to do the calibration exercises, reviews and to comment on and rate three student submissions, then review and rate their own work. This had to be completed before the time for calibration and peer review expired. When peer review was finished, students accessed the reviews of their own submissions and checked their results for their assignments. The CPR™ system managed the submission and peer review process, which freed the instructor's time towards supplying regular answers to student questions posted on the Vista site (McAlpine, Reidsema, & Allen, 2006). Rada, Michailidis and Wang (1994) suggested that peer review could reduce the instructor's workload associated with the lengthy process of providing feedback progressively on student's writing thus allowing more time for them to spend on other teaching activities. Even though there were some advantages for both the students and instructor, many students found the CPR™ process technically challenging, as they had to set up their own enrollment in a different system, which was inflexible with submission formats and dates. The system however had the advantage of being able to calibrate the reviewing skills of each student. The CPR™ system has been used at UNSW with several hundred students enrolled into the one assignment (McAlpine & Reidsema, 2007).

This CPR™ process which was adapted towards assisting students in the procedure of peer reviewing writing was designed to develop both self awareness of one's writing ability as well as the skill to rank their own and others writing against a set criteria in a collaborative environment. Carlson and Berry (2003) who have also utilised the CPR™ system in their teaching have suggested that peer review can promote higher-order thinking skills, a particularly important graduate attribute that is not always easy to accomplish in the learner. Evidence of this attribute was achieved in the Master of Art Administration research papers. During the year the CPR™ online system was utilised there were more high distinction grades (above 85%) than had been achieved in the past ten years. In the past the Research paper course was conducted using one-on-one supervision, which did not often involve providing assistance with research and writing skills.

The teaching of research methods, writing styles and ethics approved research in one semester while writing the paper has been condensed and structured to allow students to learn together online as they move through the course. My eLearning UNSW Vista provided information on research methods, writing an abstract, structuring writing, the writing process, writer's block, referencing, appendices and much other useful information as content on the WebCT Vista home page. (Refer to Figure 1 below). When students had completed the online activities and calibrated peer review of their proposal, contents page and literature review and finished their first draft, the paper was emailed to a supervisor for feedback on the content of their work before submitting the final paper. The instructional material on the Vista site and the CPR™ peer review process both assisted towards greatly reducing the amount of work and input required of the supervisor. The students utilised the discussion forum for each assignment to discuss any problems that arose, which provided a collaborative online environment where students could feel less alone as they shared their common anxieties and concerns. If problems could not be solved in this forum then students posted a group or individual question to the instructor, which were answered on a weekly basis. This time frame was implemented in order to encourage students to support each other in the learning process rather than rely so frequently on the instructor for answers to their questions.

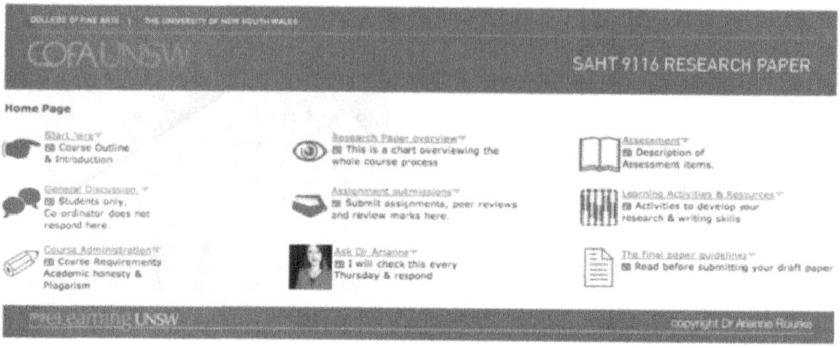

Figure 1: WebCT Vista Research Paper home page 2007

The international students in particular commented on how useful they found the structured format, guidance and feedback on their writing. Many indicated that it was unusual to receive this level of support in their Australian university studies. Many students also commented on the collaboration that evolved and the fact that they felt less isolated in the writing process while working alongside their peers. They particularly discovered that receiving feedback during the process of writing a research paper was far more useful than receiving comments after the paper was completed. The main concern students had with the CPR™ approach was that the system did not offer enough flexibility particularly with the due dates, predetermined before the semester began. They also found that the inflexible word limit provided by CPR™, which was preset by the instructor, frustrating. As a result of this student feedback the instructor decided in Semester one 2008 to remove the hyperlink to CPR™ and instead to mimic this approach to peer review as CMPR in the Discussion forum so that more flexibility could be provided.

Case study two: Using CMPR to teach how to write a research paper

During 2008 the Master of Art Administration Research paper course was run using the same format and material on WebCT Vista as the previous year but without utilising CPR™ for peer review, instead CMPR within the Vista discussion forum was adapted to mimic the CPR™ (Refer to Figure 2 below).

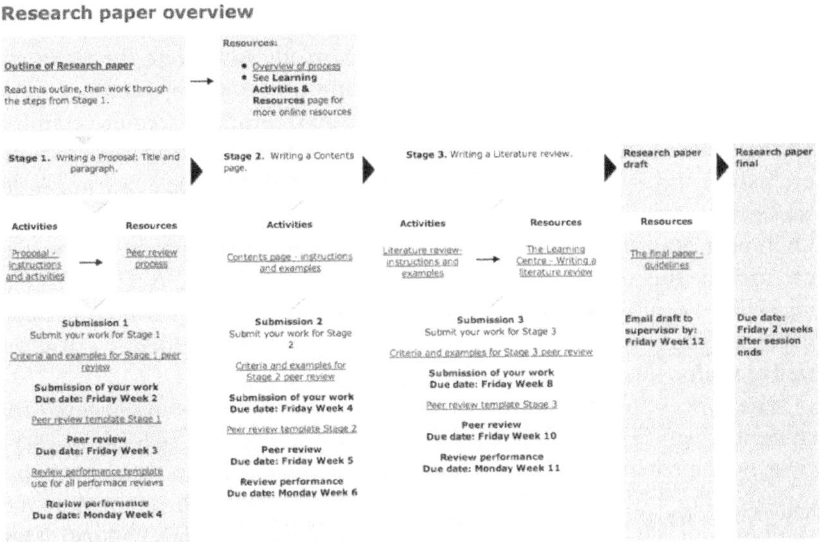

Figure 2: Overview of the research paper course using the discussion forum for peer review

As with the previous CPR™ assignments; Stage one: writing a proposal; Stage two: writing a contents page and Stage three: writing a literature review were assessed by the students. The peer review process involved two other students anonymously assessing the work completed in all three stages of writing a research paper, which were submitted for peer review to the discussion forum. To ensure that the process was fair, all students were required to look at the peer assessment examples provided on Vista. These examples demonstrated how to assess quality writing by reviewing good, medium, and poor examples of each stage, and answering questions on them. Feedback from the questions was a guide to assessment. Students then assess two submissions, followed by their own. One example of a peer review of the first stage where students submit their research proposal stated, "The content of the proposal is a very appropriate subject for research in art administration. Although this is so, the proposal lacks any definite boundaries and does not firmly conclude in a supportive reference to the hypothesis being asked. A suggestion to be made would be to more clearly define the boundaries with which this research is to be conducted, and give a clearer picture of the research subjects as a whole. This is an excellent topic that will no doubt improve awareness of gender issues within the arts administration industry." Marks were then averaged to provide a mark out of ten for each stage. The key to achieving good marks involved submitting not only a good evaluation but also paying attention to other good reviews and rating student's writing in accordance with the criteria provided. Finally students assess the effectiveness of the feedback provided by their reviewers. This process was conducted anonymously so that students could freely provide feedback in a constructive less subjective manner in the collaborative learning space. Examples of student feedback were supportive, grateful and thankful to the time and effort their peers put into reviewing with "thanks to all those who've given their time and thoughts, reviewing my work. Best wishes with those papers" and "I really appreciate the feedback you've given me for the assignments relating to the paper" (Student feedback in the discussion forum semester 2 2008). Students require training on the skills of critiquing as Brown and Knight (1995) acknowledged. "Self-evaluation and evaluation of the contribution of one's peers ... are not skills that can be undertaken without a certain amount of training" (p.52). This OCL peer review process when supported appropriately by the instructor, can provide the necessary training, constructive criticism and critical thinking skills to equip students through repeat practice, with the confidence and necessary tools to become competent assessors of other student's writing as well as their own.

The process of conducting CMPR was somewhat less complicated for students than CPR™, particularly as students did not have to log into a separate online environment and the format for submission was more straightforward. The instructor was able to be more flexible with submission and students worked from one interface in Vista (Refer to Figure 3 below). This approach relied on extensive input and ongoing planning from the instructor who was required to email students firstly their identification numbers and then progressively identification numbers of their peers for each assignment (proposal, contents page and literature review) in order for the peer review process to remain anonymous. Although the peer review format was more labour intensive for the instructor, particularly in the administration of the review process and collation of grades, which become somewhat laborious it did provide the flexibility that students had previously identified they wanted. If as "teachers we are not gaining insight into the nature of our students' learning, then we are not teaching properly. The teacher's enquiry into their students' learning is not only valuable form of educational enquiry, it is also the most valuable approach to teaching" (Rowland, 2000, p.8). It is important that the online instructor listen to the feedback of students and adjust their material, communication and assessment accordingly which should result in not only improving student learning but also enhance their satisfaction with the learning process itself.

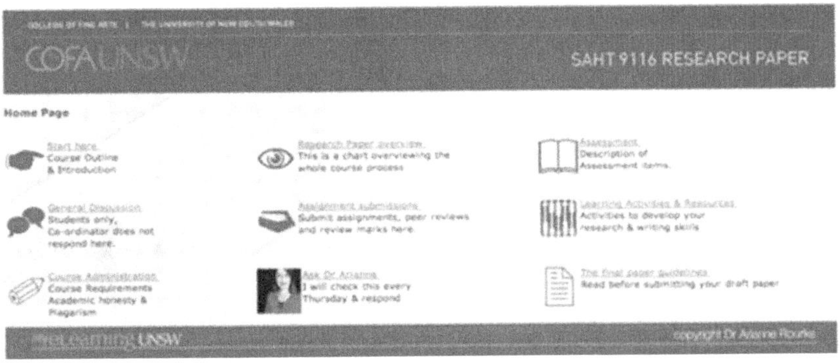

Figure 3: CMPR WebCT Vista Research Paper home page 2008

The advantage of CPR™ as previously discussed, is that it automatically randomly allocates students their peer reviewers as well as providing the instructor with a spreadsheet of marks. CMPR is, as previously mentioned, is more labour intensive for the instructor but it does offer more control and understanding of the assessment process for both the students and the educator. Student numbers for this research course are usually no more than twenty students and may have been difficult with larger cohorts of students, if this was the case the CPR™ would probably prove to be the more beneficial. CMPR through the discussion forum however, provided students with a collaborative environment to work together, alongside more personal attention from the instructor and further cooperation with peers than CPR™ as they were receiving asynchronous but individual and personal messages from the instructor and peers. As a result more individual needs were catered for in the group. The instructor also became more aware of each students individual chosen topics, writing styles and quality of reviews during each stage of the writing process rather than at the end of each stage as in CPR™ as this was visible at all stages through the forum.

Conclusion

OCL and peer review is a successful interactive tool for assisting students towards writing a successful research paper in a Postgraduate community. These processes teach students to take responsibility for their learning and become more self directed, to work cooperatively, interact in online groups and to value the opinions of others while improving time management as they work collaboratively towards a common goal. The two online collaborative peer review systems discussed in this paper provide an avenue in which the peer assessment process can become more transparent, less subjective, and by the time the awarded five marks of each task were averaged out, fairer for all students. In both the CPR™ and CMPR process students commented on the way this approach to writing a research paper gave them a sense of achievement and overall they felt less stressed about meeting deadlines as they were forced into writing earlier than they normally had in past written papers. Students also commented that breaking down the structure of the paper into stages made the paper more manageable within the fourteen-week semester period (UNSW semesters were later reduced to twelve weeks in 2008). Overall the majority of students throughout the four University semesters that the Research paper course has been running online have been positive towards the use of OCL peer review particularly as they moved from a community of coursework students in traditional face-to-face classes into individual research at the completion of the degree. They also felt they had some input into the assessment process through evaluation and feedback and they felt that their opinions were valued. The peer review process also allowed students to "become more autonomous learners able to stand on their own feet without the kind of passive dependence on the tutor for information and assessment that has been traditionally the case" (Brown & Knight, 1995, p.52).

Peer review and online collaborative learning provides ongoing support progressively throughout the process of writing a research paper. This teaching and learning process allows students to reflect and reassess their writing; learn the valuable skill of constructive reviewing of their writing and their peers as well as learning how to work collaboratively in a self directed way. As Conrad and Donaldson (2004) claimed, "reflection and self-assessment are important components for empowerment in any learner-focused environment" (p.31). All of these self and peer critiquing skills can increase students confidence in their writing ability as well as assist towards developing higher order thinking skills, an attribute highly valued in both higher education and the profession these students will be entering. In our teaching of the course, we have concluded that online courses should include in the future specific debriefing exercises at the completion where students are asked to think about their role as an assessor and reflect back on what they have learnt by participating in the collaborative peer review process.

References

Biggs, J. (1999). *Teaching for Quality Learning at University*, SHRE & Open University: Buckingham.

Boud, D. (1990) '*Assessment and the promotion of academic values*', Studies in Higher Education, 15(1), 101-11.

Bower & Richards, (2006) *Collaborative learning: Some possibilities and limitations for students and teachers.* ASCILITE 2006 Conference Proceedings.

Brookfield, S. (2006) *The skillful teacher*, Jossey-Bass: San Francisco.

Brown, G.; Bull, J. & Pendlebury, M. (1997) *Assessing students' Learning in Higher Education*, London: Routledge.

Brown S. & Knight, P. (1994) *Assessing Learners in Higher Education*, London, Philadelphia: Logan Press.

Brunk-Chevaz, B.L., & Miller, S.J. (2006). *Decentred, Disconnected and Digitized: The Importance of Shared Space*. The University of Texas El Paso & Duke University.

Bullen, M. (1998) Participation and critical thinking in on-line university distance education, *Canadian Journal of Distance Education*, 13(2), 1-32.

Carlson, P.A. & Berry, F.C. (2003). *Calibrated Peer Review and assessing learning outcomes*. Paper presented at the 33rd ASEE/IEEE Frontiers in Education Conference, Boulder, Co. USA.

Cecez-Kecmanovic, D. & Webb, C. (2000). Towards a communicative model of collaborative web-mediated learning. *Australian Journal of Educational Technology*, 16(1), 73-85. http://www.ascilite.org.au/ajet/ajet16/cecez-kecmanovic.html

Cho, K. & Schunn, C.D. (2007) *Scaffolded writing and rewriting in the discipline: A web-based reciprocal peer review system, Computers & Education*, 48 (3), 409-426.

Collins, J, Harkin, J. & Nind, M. (2002) *Manifesto for Learning*. Continuum, London & New York.

Conrad, R. & Donaldson, J. A. (2004) Engaging the online learner: Activities and resources for creative instruction. Jossey-Bass: San Francisco.

Cooper, L. (1999) *Anatomy of an online course*. THE journal 26.7:49-51. Academic Search Premier. Kennesaw State University Library, Kennesaw, GA.

Dochy, F., Segers, M. & Sluijsmans, D. (1999) *The use of Self-, Peer-, and Co-assessment in Higher Education: A Review*, Studies in Higher Education, 24(3), 331-51.

Dillenbourg, P. (2002) *Over scripting CSCL: The risk of blending collaborative learning with instructional design*. In Kirschner (Ed.) *Three Worlds of CSCL. Can we support CSCL?* Heerlen: Open University Netherlands, 64-91.

Flower, L. (1985) *Problem-solving strategies for writing*, San Diego: Harcourt Brace Jovanovich.

Guglielmo, L. (2005/6) *Teaching Composition Online*, The International Journal of Technology, Knowledge and Society. 9 (1), 103-108.

Hounsell, D. (2003) *Student feedback, learning and development*. In Slowey, M. & Watson, D. (Ed.) *Higher education and the life course*. Maidenhead: SRHE & Open University Press/McGraw-Hill, 67-78.

Lejk, M. & Wyvill, M. (2001) *The effects of the inclusion of self-assessment with peer-assessment of contributions to a group project: A quantitative study of secret and agreed assessment*. Assessment and Evaluation in Higher Education, 26(6), 551-61.

Levinsen, T, K. (2006) *Collaborative On-Line Teaching: The Inevitable Path to Deep Learning and Knowledge Sharing?* Electronic Journal of e learning, 4 (1), 41-48.

Lindblom-ylanne, Pihlajamaki & Kotkas (2006) *Self-, peer- and teacher-assessment of student essays.* Active Learning in Higher Education, 7, 51-62

Littleton, K. & Hakkinen, P. (1999) *Learning Together: Computer-based Collaborative Learning* in P. Dillenbourg (ed.) *Collaborative Learning: Cognitive and Computational Approaches.* Pergamon, Earlie, Oxford UK, 20-30.

McAlpine, I., Reidsema, C., & Allen, B. (2006). *Educational design and online support for an innovative project-based course in engineering design.* Proceedings of the 23rd annual conference of the Australasian Society for Computers in Learning in Tertiary Education, Sydney University Press: Sydney, 497-507.

McAlpine, I. & Reidsema, C. (2007). *The Role of Student Peer Review and Assessment in an Introductory Project-Based Engineering Design Course.* Connect-Ed International Conference on Design Education.

Mulder, R.A. & Pearce, J.M. (2007). *PRAZE: innovating teaching through online peer review. In ICT: Providing choices for learners and learning.* Proceedings ASCILITE Singapore 2007.

Orsmond, P., Merry, S,. Reiling, K. (1996). *The Importance of Marking Criteria in the Use of Peer Assessment in* Assessment & Evaluation in Higher Education, **21**[3], 239-250.

Orsmond, P., Merry, S,. Reiling, K. (1997). *A study in Self Assessment: Tutor and Students' perceptions of performance* in Assessment & Evaluation in Higher Education, **22** [4], pp 357-369.

Orsmond, P., S. Merry and K. Reiling (2000). "The Use of Student Derived Marking Criteria in Peer and Self-Assessment." *Assessment and Evaluation in Higher Education* 25 (1): 23-38.

Orsmond, P., Merry, S. & Reiling, K. (2002) The use of formative feedback when using student derived marking criteria in peer and self assessment, Assessment & Evaluation in Higher Education, 27(4), pp.309-323.

Powers, M., Guan, S. (2000) *Examining the Range of Student Needs in the Design and development of Web-based Course.* In Abbey, B. (Ed.) *Instructional and Cognitive Impacts of Web-Based Education*, Ideal Group Publishing: London.

Raadt de, M., Toleman, M. & Watson, R. (2005). *Electronic Peer Review: A large cohort teaching themselves?* ASCILITE 2005 Conference proceedings.

Rada, R. Michailidis, A. & Wang, W (1994) *Collaborative hypermedia in a classroom setting.* Journal of Educational Multimedia and Hypermedia, 3(1), 21-36.

Rourke, Mendelssohn, Coleman (2008) *Peer Review and the Coursework Postgraduate: Two case studies from the Master of Art Administration at COFA, UNSW'*. The International Journal of Learning, 14 (12), 7-12.

Rowland, S. (2000) *The Enquiring University Teacher*, SRHE and Open University Press: Buckingham.

Segers, M. & Dochy, F. (2001) *New assessment forms in Problem-based learning: The value added of the students' perspective*. Studies in Higher Education, 26(3), 327-43.

Struyven, K., Dochy, F. & Janssens (2005) *Students' perceptions about evaluation and assessment in higher education: a review, Assessment & Evaluation*. Higher Education, 30(4) 325 – 341.

Topping, K. (1998). *Peer Assessment Between Students in Colleges and Universities*. Review of Educational Research, 68(3), 249-276.

Topping, K.; Smith, E.; Swanson, I. & Elliot, A. (2000) *Formative Peer Assessment of Academic Writing Between Postgraduate Students*. Assessment and Evaluation in Higher Education, 25(2), 149-69.

Collaborating with Wikis in the Instructional Design Process

James A. West

This case study examined the online collaboration efforts of students in a multimedia instructional design course. Collaborative writing tools, such as wikis, are well suited to supporting meaningful learning and promoting critical thinking. Wikis offer a shared environment where students can actively participate in the integration and co-creation of knowledge. Wiki technology can be harnessed to foster dynamic online learning communities where students come together around a shared goal. Wiki community members use the shared space to write, discuss, comment, edit, reflect, evaluate, and ultimately complete a shared outcome. While wikis hold great promise for learning, without planning, design, and effective facilitation, a wiki is no more than an empty web page. The purpose of the case study was to determine how well students actually collaborated using a wiki. Students were provided a rich scenario involving multiple departments and colleges across campus. Observations of collaborative activity were made, and the quality of group outcomes was measured. Student reactions were generally positive: online collaboration tools helped them work together to meet group goals. In addition, the wiki environment helped to assuage typical fears of group projects, such as division of group work and non-participation of individual group members.

Introduction

There is no doubt that the World Wide Web is changing. Since the turn of the 21st century, the once static Web has evolved into the "Read/Write

Web" (Richardson, 2006) offering new opportunities for learning, teaching, and collaboration. Growth of so called Web 2.0 tools such as Blogs and Wikis is astounding, with new collaborative tools coming online almost daily. For online educators, there is growing interest in discovering ways to effectively harness these technologies to improve learning and promote the construction of a collaborative knowledge base.

Web 2.0 tools, in particular collaborative tools such as Wikis, are well suited for supporting the concept of "open source learning." Open source learning is participatory and collects knowledge and resources from diverse perspectives. It can be harnessed to foster a dynamic learning culture that allows students to create, review, reflect, evaluate, and modify the knowledge and outcomes of a group. Online educators must learn to embrace this "age of participation" using the low-cost infrastructure of the Web and to effectively coach students in their ability to collaborate online in the creation of products, information, and learning (Tapscott and Williams, 2007).

A wiki can provide the tools and the collaborative work space that enables contextual teaching and learning. The online educator builds on the wiki environment and adds context and purpose through:

- Establishing a purpose for the wiki experience
- Defining and classifying learning goals by domain
- Designing a rich context and problem (specifically a "wiki frame") that supports the achievement of the purpose and goals
- Promoting a collaborative environment where active, social learning can take place

Literature Review

The ultimate goal of online education is to provide experiences to students that lead to meaningful learning. Educators today understand that meaningful learning cannot be accomplished solely through passive activities such as reading and listening. According to constructivist theory, meaning is gained through active learning, social interaction, and the construction of knowledge (see, for example, Bruner, 1990; Fink, 2003; Jonassen, Howland, Marra, & Crismond, 2007).

Constructivist theory also suggests that meaningful learning is dependent on a rich and relevant context. Contextual Teaching and Learning, an instructional systems theory that schools and higher educational reform movements are steadily adopting, is "based on the premise that meaning emerges from the relationship between content and its context. Context gives meaning to content" (Johnson, 2002, p. 3). As such, according to contextual teaching and learning principles, the role of the instructor is not to provide learning. The role of the instructor is to provide the context in which learning can occur. Contextual teaching and learning engages students in signifi cant and relevant activities that help them connect their academic learning to real - life situations and problems.

Online educators already know that successful online collaboration does not come easily (Palloff & Pratt, 2005). While online courses "bring together [students] who might not otherwise be able to work together due to time, travel, and cost restrictions," online students face a variety of challenges over their face-to-face counterparts (Buono, 2004). Couple the challenges of learning online with the challenges of group work, and you have a double-whammy. Given these factors, simply making a wiki or set of online collaborative writing tools available to online students is not enough. In fact, in one study, student groups were given an empty wiki as a group workspace with no structure or direction, and only a few groups used the wiki at all (Mindel and Verma, 2006). Online educators need to consider both the desired outcomes of the learning and the process of wiki collaboration when planning and facilitating a wiki project. In order to ensure positive learning outcomes, educators must consider the learning domain and know how to effectively frame wiki activities that lead to meaningful learning. In order to master the process, educators must know how to effectively prepare students for wiki collaboration, facilitate group progress, and manage conflicts and distractions.

Students collaborating online face a variety of challenges different from their experiences in face-to-face groups (Buono, 2004). Without context and support, online groups can experience unbalanced participation, a lack of progress and direction, mistrust, misunderstandings, and confl icts. Given these factors, simply making an empty wiki available to online students is not enough (Mindel & Verma, 2006). A successful wiki project must take into account the learning outcomes and goals of the project and the unique process of wiki collaboration. Educators must know how to frame wiki activities such that they lead to meaningful learning. During the process of collaboration, educators must learn to take facilitative roles, in which they prepare students for wiki collaboration, facilitate group progress, and manage confl icts and distractions.

Johnson (2002) suggests that when students are provided with a rich context and the tools for learning, they achieve higher levels of learning, see a stronger relevance between the problems in the classroom and the problems of the real world, and are more satisfied with the learning experience. When students formulate projects or identify interesting problems, when they make choices and accept responsibility, when they search out information and reach conclusions, when they actively choose, order, organize, touch, plan, investigate, question, and make decisions to reach objectives, they connect academic content to the context of life ' s situations, and in this way discover meaning.

As students mature and advance in their learning, it becomes necessary for you to give them opportunities to apply and transfer their developing skills to a variety of new problems and situations. Skills, to be durable, must be portable and transferable outside of the protective walls of the classroom. Learning experiences must encourage students to CREATE and DO, not just think. On Bloom's Taxonomy (Bloom, 1956; Anderson &

Krathwohl, 2001), these learning outcomes are best represented by the domains of Applying (for example, experimenting, planning, mapping) and Creating (for example, designing, composing, integrating).

Contextual learning is based on the premise that learning and meaning emerge from the relationship between content and context. It is the context (the environment or problem) that gives meaning to the content (Johnson, 2002). Contextual teaching and learning engage students in signifi cant activities — in rich learning environments — that help them connect their academic learning to real - life situations and problems.

Background and Case Study Questions

IDT 440 centers on the design and development of a multimedia instructional product, either for the web or CD-ROM. These media design projects are typically group efforts that focus on identifying a need and designing an appropriate solution to meet that need. These projects are meant to model real - world group processes. Unfortunately, the benefits of having students complete these types of collaborative projects often come with challenges of their. Students may complain that "So-and-so didn't do anything on the project, but got the same grade as me," or "If I had been able to work on the project I would have fixed all the problems and we could have gotten a better grade."

Media design projects have the potential to work well in wikis, which allow group members to monitor the project, conduct reviews, provide feedback to members, and maintain balanced participation and version control. In addition, using a wiki can also provide the structure for monitoring group processes that will help overcome many of the complaints students may have with group project.

To guide the thinking around this case study, it was useful to develop several questions about the project:

1. Compared to other group projects, did working in a wiki help you in your collaboration processes?
2. What were the benefits of collaborating in a wiki?
3. What were the challenges you faced in working in a wiki?

Using Wikis for Media Design Projects

Preparing students to wiki begins even before the first day of the online course. Preparation includes managing student expectations, stimulating relevant skills and attitudes, and orienting students to the new learning environment. Wiki preparation strategies can be integrated into the precourse activities many online instructors are already using. The wiki is used as a scaffold or support structure for every aspect of the group process from formation through the accomplishment of group goals. Wiki projects such as team-based design, scripting, and storyboarding have been effectively supported through the use of wikis (West, Sample & West, 2007).

A media design project must include the necessary documentation and steps required to move the project through the stages of analysis, design, and development. The wiki can be used as the center for collaborating on key planning documents, including the needs assessment, audience analysis, scripts, and storyboards. The wiki serves as the central location for all of the relevant documents, and can also provide a means for group members to share files, comment on progress, and manage the project. In IDT 440, it is important for students to share their project files with other stakeholders, such as clients, managers, and the instructor. The wiki serves as a central location for both writing project documentation and file sharing. Although media design projects can vary in length and scope, typically they will include:

- Analysis documents
- Proposals and scope documents
- Design documents
- Storyboards or scripts
- Evaluation documents

The Wiki Frame for IDT 440

The Fall 2008 IDT 440 class was approached by the Instructor of English 202: Introduction to Drama. The instructor teaches a unit on what goes on behind the scenes in the production of a play. It was determined that a multimedia program that demonstrated the various aspects of producing a play would help students in this class. Based on interviews with the instructor, the multimedia program would focus on four main areas: Key Roles in Producing a Play; Lighting and Audio; Costumes, Props, and Staging; and Acting and Directing. Based on these four areas, the IDT 440 class was divided into four groups, one for each area of the program. Each group selected a group leader, and one student was elected to be the project manager across all four groups.

The wiki was structured around these four groups. The wiki home page included a description of the project, notes on how and when to post to the wiki, and names of each of the groups working on the project. Each group was given a folder in which they could create pages, upload files, and share comments. For each group, a wiki frame was set up around the five stages in the design process listed above. Students were able to view any page in the wiki, but could only create and edit documents in the folder for the group to which they were assigned. Students were required to write and edit their group documents in the wiki. No paper copies were ever submitted to the instructor.

Monitoring Group Outcomes and Processes

The wiki provided several different ways of monitoring student activity as they progressed through the project. First, as is typical of many wikis, the wiki maintained copies of all versions of documents written in the wiki. This is an important distinction and benefit of wikis. Rather than maintaining various word processed documents, and trying to control who has the most current version, pages written in the wiki automatically store all previous versions of the documents. The most current version of any document is always available to anyone in the group for editing or reviewing. This version control also provided a means to track how often each person in the group contributed to the overall final version of their documents. It was clear, both to the instructor and to the students, who was participating and who was not.

Second, the wiki's comment area was used both for students to communicate with each on their progress and to confirm participation in the group's process of writing and collaboration. For each document, group members were required to state that they had read and approved the final version submitted to the instructor for grading. The purpose of this step was to reduce the possibility of complaints regarding group input. Students who did not "sign off" on the project were given less credit. No one was allowed to blame the failure of a project on someone else's work.

Third, to reduce the possibility of students signing off without actually participating or even reading the documents, each time a document was due was followed with a quiz on specific details of the group's document.

By setting up the project this way, it allowed the instructor to grade each project outcomes "as is" (that is, each student in the group received the same grade on the project itself), while allowing individual grading on the project process.

Student Reactions to Collaborating Online

After the completion of the course, students were interviewed to see their reactions to group collaboration using a wiki. In general, students felt that the wiki helped them collaborate better. They thought that it was easier to provide input into their group's project. One key aspect for the students was that it helped them overcome scheduling conflicts which commonly occurred to them in group assignments for other courses.

Students noted some technical advantages to using the wiki. Version control was very valuable, both in that it made each person's contributions apparent to everyone in the group as well as the instructor, and it made it easy to restore previous versions in case of accidental changes to previously written material. Table 1 summarizes the benefits that students reported in collaborating in a wiki.

Table 1: Benefits of Collaborating in a Wiki

• Resolved scheduling conflicts
• Other group member's contributions are clear visible
• History option allowed you to recover previous work
• Discussion boards
• Email updates of changes
• Changes show up immediately
• Easy to learn
• Group folder capabilities were useful
• The wiki provided peer pressure to make sure you contributed

The students did have some challenges in working with the wiki. In terms of collaboration, some students felt that the wiki allowed others to sit back and watch rather than participate with the group. Collaborating in the wiki, rather than in face-to-face meetings meant that students had to get in the habit of checking their group's wiki pages. Another challenge was getting used to editing what someone else had written. Students in this class were used to group projects in which they could "divide and conquer" and then patch everything together at the end.

Several challenges revolved around technical difficulties with the wiki. Although email alerts were helpful, sometimes it was overwhelming because whenever a member of any group made a change, everyone in the class received an email alert, regardless of which group updated their pages. In addition, the wiki's editing tools were not as powerful as what students were used to compared with Microsoft Word. In addition, the additional features such as uploading files were not always easy to figure out. Table 2 summarizes some of the key challenges that students expressed in working with the wiki.

Table 2: Challenges of Collaborating in a Wiki and Suggestions for Further Research

Need more control over email alerts
Some students could lay back and watch rather than pitch in
Special features were confusing to use
Formatting documents was not as easy as using a word processing program

Conclusion

Case studies are a good way of providing discussion around details of a specific instance or case under investigation. In this case study, student reactions to collaborating using a wiki were, for the most part, very positive. One outcome of the study for the instructor was that there were fewer complaints at the end of the semester that some students received grades higher or lower than they deserved. Students felt that some aspects of the process could be improved, such as being able to select their own group members or develop their own project ideas. However, since these were not a function of using the wiki, this may be a complaint about group work in general that this case study did not address.

Ideally, the wiki should be used because it is an appropriate tool for the learning requirements of the project. In this case, the wiki appeared to provide the structure and support the students needed to be successful in the course.

Areas for further study include reporting statistical data can be captured showing how often students contributed to their pages, and the overall quality of their group's work. In addition, comparing groups that are using a wiki with groups that work in a more traditional, face-to-face atmosphere could help to shed light on when best to use this technology for future collaborative work.

References

Anderson, L.W. & Krathwohl, D.R. (Eds.) (2001) A taxonomy for learning, teaching and assessing: A revision of Bloom's taxonomy of educational objectives. New York: Longman.

Bloom, B.S. (Ed.) (1956) Taxonomy of educational objectives: The classification of education goals: Handbook I, cognitive domain. New York; Toronto: Longmans, Green.

Bruner, J. (1990). Acts of meaning. Cambridge, MA: Harvard University Press.

Buono, A. F. (2004) "Leadership challenges in global virtual teams: lessons from the field," SAM Advanced Management Journal. 69(4), pp. 4-10.

Fink, L. D. (2003). Creating Significant Learning Experiences: An Integrated Approach to Designing College Courses. San Francisco, CA: Jossey-Bass.

Johnson, E. B. (2002) Contextual teaching and learning: What it is and why it's here to stay. Thousand Oaks, CA: Sage Publications.

Jonassen, D.H., Howland, J., Marra, R.M., & Crismond, D. (2007). Meaningful learning with technology, 3rd Ed. Columbus, OH: Merrill/Prentice Hall.

Mindel, J. L. & Verma, S. (2006) "Wikis for teaching and learning," Communications of the Association for Information Systems. 18(1), pp. 1-23.

Palloff, R. M. & Pratt, K. (2005) Collaborating online: Learning together in community. San Francisco, CA: Jossey-Bass.

Richardson, W. (2006). Blogs, wikis, podcasts and other powerful Web tools for classrooms. Thousand Oaks, CA: Corwin Press.

Tapscott, D., & Williams, A. (2006). Wikinomics: How mass collaboration changes everything. New York: Portfolio Hardcover (Penguin).

West, J., Sample, S., and West, M. (2007). Online Collaboration Tools in Instructional Design. Selected Papers from the 2007 Annual Conference on Distance Teaching and Learning. Madison, WI.

Part IV

Conclusion

The Reflective Practitioner

Arianne Rourke and Kathryn Coleman

This edited collection of best practice has presented a selection of reflective practitioners and their teaching practice that provides exemplars of where 'pedagogy leads the technology' in the academic world where the opposite is often promoted and supported. The role of the reflective practitioner in higher education is to investigate their teaching in order to improve their students learning outcomes. Paramount to this is 'recognising' the value of learning from experience as well as the importance of providing new learning enterprises that assist the learner to link their past knowledge and experience to new knowledge. We believe as Glowacki-Dudka & Barnett, (2007) put forward that: "reflective practice is not only useful for individuals, but it becomes critical when it is applied within organizations and communities to examine the collective assumptions of the work" (p. 43). Reflecting on one's teaching practice is an essential part of the 'professionalism' of teaching, which is particularly important in the online environment where as a time and labour saving mechanism courses are often rolled-over from Semester to Semester and the technology is rolled out with little consideration towards the pedagogy of teaching and student learning.

According to Cross (2009) "professional teachers seek to communicate their field of knowledge... in such a way that the learner is nurtured, supported and able to develop" (p. 161), which relies on the fact that the educators not only understand what teaching methods to adopt but they also have an inkling of their students preferred learning styles and background knowledge that could assist them in the learning process. These factors apply whether teaching in the f2f classroom, or in a blended or fully online course, the pedagogy of teaching needs to be at the forefront of the educators mind when writing, designing, implementing and reviewing courses.

As the case studies of good practice presented in this book exemplify, it is not enough to provide information, discussion forums and links to websites, educators have to design instructional learning activities that promote active learning and collaboration as well as providing the learner with a sense of ownership of the learning process.

Another factor behind this perspective is the recognition of the importance of promoting a nexus between theory and practice, as well as the connections between teaching and research. As Ashcroft & Foreman-Peck (1994) recommended, the critical part of reflective practice is that it requires a commitment to learning from experience and from evidence, rather than to learning certain 'recipes' for action" (p.3). Hence the reflective practitioner takes into account that there is many factors that inform their teaching practice whether online or f2f. These include but are not exclusive to: reading the literature on teaching and learning; developing your philosophy of teaching and learning; learning from ones own learning experience; being aware of the student's own perspective on learning; the teachers grasp and views on the acquisition of disciplinary knowledge and understanding; the role of assessment for learning as well as the need to develop graduate attributes to name but a few. Biggs (1999) suggested that: "reflecting on your teaching, and seeing what is wrong and how it may be improved, requires you to have an explicit theory of teaching" (p.6).

The reflective practitioner ultimately through further understanding their own teaching and their student's learning and by being receptive to other's philosophical stances, develop a theoretical perspective that enhance their understanding of their professional teaching practice. According to Brookfield (2005), "a theory is nothing more or less than a set of explanatory understandings that help us to make sense of some aspects of the world" (p.3) involving "interpreting, predicting, explaining" (p.3). As Cross (2009) believed a "sound understanding of theory is essential to the development of a teaching professional" (p.3). Applying, extending and ultimately challenging theory has always been an important aspect of both the editors' teaching practice and research. In order to be a reflective practitioner you have to also become aware that there are no prescriptive answers to describe the best way of teaching students to learn in the f2f classroom or in the online environment in higher education. In some cases this can take years of practice and dedication to the 'art' of teaching as you work through to advance from a novice to an expert teacher.

As Korthagen (2001) suggested, an important function of reflection is to assist teachers "to become aware of their mentals structures, subject them to critical analysis, and if necessary restructure them" (p.51). Being aware of ones mental structuring of knowledge and experience of teaching and learning involves becoming educators who are participants in life-long learning. It also involves being dedicated to the profession of teaching and being prepared to scrutinise where changes can be implemented to improve both teaching and student learning. The reflective practitioner recognises that this is an ongoing, never ending process and they are dedicated to this continuum in their professional teaching careers. As many researchers have acknowledged, reflection is a continuous cycle (Kolb & Fry, 1975; Boud, Keogh & Walker, 1985) and the reflective practitioner is prepared to nurture and sustain this evolving process as they invest time and energy into further fostering their interests in teaching and student learning.

Most importantly educators in higher education need to sustain the belief that as teachers and educational researchers, we can have a positive impact on both teaching and student learning outcomes. Korthagen (2001) defined reflection as the "mental process of trying to (re) structure an experience, a problem or existing knowledge or insights" (p.58). Foremost in the mind of the reflective practitioner is that teaching and their student's engagement in the learning process can always improve. Evidence based research can assist the teacher towards discovering invaluable insights into student learning and improving pedagogy so that justifiable changes can be made in the classroom to further promote student learning.

It is important in teaching in higher education that educators attempt to view the learning process from the learner's perspective and to recognise when there are barriers to student learning and to reflect on their teaching practice in order to discover ways of assisting the learner to overcome these barriers. Teaching 'fads' in elearning can be persuaders of adoption, as Schön (1983, 1987) advocated, reflection is an important part of the learning process as reflectivity allows the student or educator to see the fundamental relationship between their actions and their framing of the situation, rather than jumping from new learning tool to learning tool. Davis (2003) has however added the voice of realism to the argument with the view that academics feel "de-motivated" because of "lack of resources, lack of recognition, overwork and lack of appreciation" (p.243). Davis (2003) also suggested that, "universal reflective practice may come in the long term but only once the deeper-seated problems within the sector (who value research over teaching) are resolved" (p.243).

In order to obtain a balanced view on such concerns, it is important that educators take into account the perspective of other colleagues who have provided invaluable insights and support, which can in-turn inform their own reflective practice. Such collaborations through team teaching and researching could assist towards further promoting within the higher education sector the importance of developing a strong nexus between teaching and research. As Carr and Kemmis (1986) and Cochran-Smith and Lytle (1999) argued, there is a need to work towards the establishment of collaborative teacher professional learning communities and the development of research in relation to them. As this book has showcased, this is happening successfully in many educational institutions around the world. These educators have reflected on their practice and their students learning and used this knowledge and understanding to design, develop and deliver exceptional online learning and teaching that has provided valuable exemplars of 'pedagogy leading the technology' for other educators to follow.

An educators' reflective practice seeks to further develop the scholarship of teaching. The editors' have selected the research papers contained in this book to provide multiple perspectives on new pedagogies in online learning and teaching. As Reeves and Herrington (2010) concur, research into instructional design is imperative if the field of research is to further grow and evolve out of research and into practice. As Johnson & Warren (2007) found, it is now time to move "beyond questioning whether the new learning technologies can contribute to an improvement over traditional methods" (p.2). It is time to present what works and let new researchers continue to build on these foundations.

For many educators' the move to fully online or blended learning has been fraught with difficulties. Many Learning institutions are now however, fully equipped for online learning and teaching and elearning is common practice in education in the 21st Century. Desktop computers, laptops, netbooks and iPads are in the hands of most teaching faculty, presentation halls, lecture theatres and tutorials which are now days are fully equipped for online material to be presented. Some institutions have moved beyond traditional classrooms to more contemporary learning spaces, constructivist in nature, offering students collaborative work stations for group and peer assessment. As these practices continue to be supported by administrators, this is the perfect time to ensure the linking of pedagogy and technology and learner needs in online curriculum. Much of the literature has been about student achievement and student satisfaction as a means of assessing the value of elearning. It is now time to reflect on all this research into addressing emerging technologies, educational theories and move beyond discussing embedding technology and discuss its practice so that researchers and educators' can 'stand on the shoulders of giants'.

References:

Ashcroft, K. & Foreman-Peck, L. (1994). *Managing teaching and learning in Further and Higher Education*, London: Flamer.

Biggs, J. (1999). *Teaching for quality learning at University*, Buckingham & Philadelphia: SRHE & Open University.

Boud, D., Keogh, R., & Walker, D. (1985). Promoting reflection in learning : a model. In D. Boud, R. Keogh, & D. walker (Eds.), *Reflection: Turning Experience into Learning* (pp.18-40). London, Kogan Page.

Brookfeild, S. (2005). *The Power of Critical Theory for Adult Learning and Teaching*, San Francisco, CA: Jossey-Bass.

Carr, W. & Kemmis, S. (1986). *Becoming critical: Education, Knowledge and Action Research*, Geelong: Deakin University Press.

Cochran-Smith & Lytle, S. L. (1999). Teacher learning in professional communities: three knowledge-practice relationships in P.Pearson & A. Iran-Nejad (Eds.) *Review of Research in Education*, pp.251-307, Washington, DC: American educational Research Association.

Cross, S. (2009). *Adult Teaching and Learning, Developing your Practice*, Berkshire, England: Open University Press.

Davis, D. (2003). Barriers to reflective practice. *Active Learning in Higher Education*, 4(3), 243-255.

Glowacki-Dudka, M. & Barnett, N. (2007), Connecting Critical reflection and Group Development in Online Adult Education Classrooms. 19 (1), 43-53.

Kolb. D. A. and Fry, R. (1975) Toward an applied theory of experiential learning;, in C. Cooper (ed.) *Theories of Group Process*, London: John Wiley.

Korthagen, F.A.J. (2001). *Linking Practice and Theory, The Pedagogy of Realistic Teaching Education*, Mahwah, New Jersey: Lawrence Erlbaum.

Schön, D.A. (1983). *The Reflective Practitioner*, San Francisco: Jossey-Bass.

Schön, D.A. (1987). *Educating the Reflective Practitioner*, San Francisco: Jossey-Bass.

CPSIA information can be obtained at www.ICGtesting.com
Printed in the USA
LVOW010233180413

329743LV00002B/31/P

9 781863 359146